ILLUMINATED BY WATER

ILLUMINATED BY WATER

Fly Fishing and the
Allure of the Natural World

MALACHY TALLACK

PEGASUS BOOKS

NEW YORK LONDON

ILLUMINATED BY WATER

Pegasus Books, Ltd.
148 West 37th Street, 13th Floor
New York, NY 10018

First Pegasus Books cloth edition August 2022

The author and publisher would gratefully like to acknowledge The University of Chicago Press for permission to quote from *A River Runs Through It* by Norman Maclean, ©1976 by the University of Chicago.

ISBN: 978-1-63936-165-6

10 9 8 7 6 5 4 3 2 1

Printed in the United States of America
Distributed by Simon & Schuster
www.pegasusbooks.com

For Rory

CONTENTS

INTRODUCTION

FROM THE SQUAT CONCRETE BRIDGE, humming with Saturday traffic, we took the towpath east along the Forth and Clyde Canal. It was mid-morning, mid-November, and the air was chilly and damp. I guessed we would get rained on before our walk was done. The clouds had that look about them: dark around the edges, like eyes in need of sleep.

Beyond a busy marina, packed with cruisers and narrowboats – some lived in, some swaddled in tarpaulin for the winter – things grew quiet. A few joggers, dog walkers and a cyclist or two, but we were mostly on our own. Shoulder to shoulder on the narrow path, my partner, Roxani, took the side with the trees and grassy banks, and I took the side with the water.

I like canals, as a general rule. I like the way they are not quite one thing or another. In form, they take the shape of rivers, but in habit and as habitat they are lakes, stretched out across the landscape. Few things we humans build for our own convenience do much to assist the natural world. But canals, cleaned up, have become an exception. Insects, amphibians, fish, birds and mammals all make their homes in and around the water. Canals once helped sustain the industrial economy of this country. Now they help sustain other kinds of life.

This one, as its name suggests, connects the Firth of Forth in the east to the Firth of Clyde in the west, bisecting Scotland at its narrowest point. Thirty-five miles in length, it was opened in 1790, joining sea to sea and city to city. Glasgow lies at one end, Falkirk at the other; and until 1933, a series of locks provided a further link, through the Union Canal, to Edinburgh. Today, the Falkirk Wheel does the same job, but with added drama.

At the water's edge, thick beds of bulrushes and reeds provide cover for birds. Not many, on that day, just a few pairs of mallards, idling in the shallows, and a mottled grey cygnet, begging for bread. On the opposite bank were moorhens, emerging and vanishing among the vegetation, announcing themselves testily with brassy toots and honks.

Like a lot of the walks Roxani and I take together, this one was partly an excuse to be near water, and that proximity was an excuse to look for and wonder about the lives within. Almost everything along the canal led the eye in the opposite direction. The trees pointed upwards, and so did the spires of rushes and dried angelica. There were the flocks of fieldfares that came and went in gusts; there was the young buzzard that flapped one way, and the female sparrowhawk that coasted the other. Even the water faced away from itself, the still surface reflecting the bare branches on the other bank and the pallid sky above. Like all mirrors, it was hiding as much as it revealed.

Beyond a second bridge, a man with two fishing rods on the bank, lines already in the water, was casting a third as we passed. Attached was a chunky white float, and dangling beneath it, a fish. Silver and finger-length, it was long dead, most likely. There are pike in this canal – ravenous hunters, always looking for an easy meal – for which that would be the perfect bait. The man flicked the rod gently over his shoulder, and fish and float came down with a splash.

A little farther along, we passed another angler, just setting up. This one was accompanied by a young woman, hunched by the water in a canvas chair, staring at her phone. He, meanwhile, was threading line unhurriedly through the eyes of his rod, a carton of maggots open at his feet and a joint clenched between his teeth. He grinned at us as we passed, and the sweet stink of marijuana sprawled out along the towpath.

I had read up before we got there. I wanted to know what kinds of fish lived in the canal, even though I wouldn't be fishing. I wanted to be able to imagine, to look at the water and wonder. In truth, I would happily have stopped to watch one or other of the anglers, just stood and waited for an hour or two to see what they caught; but I suspect neither one of them (and nor, perhaps, Roxani) would have approved. As we walked, though, I searched for evidence, scanning for signs of life below. A single, subtle 'rise': the concentric ripples that appear when a fish takes food – an insect, most often – from the surface. A necklace of bubbles, belched by a tench or bream. A shuddering among reeds, which could, really, have been almost anything. Each hint, each detail, brought a momentary lurch of excitement, a thrill that had me peering, heron-like, into the murk.

That urgency of the almost-seen is with me whenever I am near water. It is like the aftermath of a shooting star, as your eyes clutch at the darkness for another, or like the last moments of anticipation for long-deferred news. It is waiting, questioning, hankering.

The appeal of angling is sometimes explained away as a 'hunting instinct', as though such a thing, if it truly existed, would be a simple matter. But I am not convinced. For me, the desire to catch fish is the opposite of simple, and at its root is not an eagerness to kill or to capture at all. If forced to pare it down, I would point instead to a quite different instinct: an intense, focused curiosity. What I feel beside water is the urge to uncover what is hidden, the urge to see and hold what is otherwise only glimpsed, or else never seen at all. It is the longing to look through that mirrored surface and to know for certain what is down there. That longing can transform a life. It can turn all water into a place of wonder.

Between one and two million people go fishing in the UK each year, and in the United States the numbers are much higher: around 35 million anglers annually, according to the US Fish and Wildlife Service. That's a significant proportion of the population of both countries, for whom the lure of the aquatic is at least occasionally irresistible. Some of these people, naturally, will be once-only anglers, dragged along by an enthusiastic parent or partner. But for many of them, fishing is something very important indeed.

I am an angler, and I have been an angler since I was young. Few other labels sit so comfortably with me. Few can be applied, as this one can, without qualification. Angling is tangled in my memories, my daydreams and my ambitions. It has shaped the way I look at and notice the world, and the way I think about my place within it. It is the childhood obsession that failed to fade, the youthful fervour that never fully let me go. While almost everything else has changed in the years since I first went fishing, I can still find that same surge of adventure that drew me in and hooked me, more than three decades ago. Angling – and *thinking* about angling – has been a precious constant in my life, even at times when I've fished less often than I've wanted to. Like listening again to the songs I loved as a teenager, each return to the water feels like a return to myself.

The poet and novelist Jim Harrison once wrote that 'fishing is the activity that ensures my sanity', and I know pretty much what he meant. Angling has a steadying effect for me, not just when I am there, casting or catching, but at other times too, remembering, imagining. It offers a connection to place that feels more intimate and multifaceted than most, and an engagement with the natural world that is knotty and compelling. It is an engagement of attention, certainly, but also an involvement in the lives – and sometimes the deaths – of those creatures the angler pursues.

Like all hobbies, angling is both a way of wasting time and, simultaneously, a way of generating meaning from that time. Ailm Travler has written that 'fishing is folly: useless, unreasonable, irrational, and without purpose'. But she doesn't mean this as criticism. After all, how many of life's great pleasures are likewise useless? How much of what is most important is also without purpose? As Travler puts it, 'fishing is folly precisely because it makes survival harder than it already is, and by doing so, turns survival into an art'. It isn't necessary to feel certain about that word, 'art', in order to take her point: that angling creates its own kind of meaning, its own kind of significance. It is, she concludes, 'evocative beyond thought – the rings of water after a rise'.

This book is an attempt to trace some of those rings, to follow them outwards and to see where they go. It is an attempt to grasp some of that meaning and that significance. This is a book about angling, but it is also about rivers, lakes and canals, and the things that live in and around them. It is about beauty, about hope, and about how freedom is sought and sometimes found. It is a book not just for those who already fish and who therefore understand what it is to cast a line, but for those who are curious, and who wish to know more about the places that fishing can take you.

There is a long-established relationship between angling and writing, the end product of which are the countless books that have been published on the subject, and that continue to be published today. Few pastimes, surely, have attracted quite so many words over the centuries. The most famous of these books, without question, is Izaak Walton's *The Compleat Angler*, which first appeared in 1653, and which is reputed to be the third most reprinted book in the English language, after the Bible and the Book of Common Prayer (though I have yet to see evidence for this oft-repeated claim).

Walton's treatise was written in the wake of the English Civil War, in which he, as an Anglican and a Royalist, was on the losing side. It was a violent, tumultuous time, and Walton had put his own life at risk, smuggling one of the Crown Jewels to London after the Battle of Worcester in 1651. Yet, in his book, he turned away from the turmoil of the world towards the peace and the joyfulness that he found beside water. 'No life, my honest scholar,' he wrote, 'no life so happy and so pleasant as the life of a well-governed angler.'

Walton believed that angling was a virtuous activity – 'the most honest, ingenuous, quiet, and harmless art' – and that, in turn, it promoted good virtues among its practitioners. No wonder, he argued, that Jesus picked four fishermen to be among his disciples, for they were 'men of mild, and sweet, and peaceable spirits'. Indeed, the ultimate conclusion of the book's many (and occasionally somewhat tiresome) philosophical and theological digressions is that fishiness is next to godliness. Or something like that. And the source of angling's virtue, as far as Walton was concerned? It is an *action* that promotes *contemplation*, that provides, indeed, the ideal balance between body and mind.

I'm not certain whether angling has made me a better man, whether it has lifted my morals in any meaningful way. I'd like to think so, but I fear Walton was mistaken. Deluded, even. His efforts to justify the sport, though moderated by the cheerful humility that was his hall-mark, have a definite air of defensiveness, and of sanctimony, too. Walton was a man who, having just lost a war, was desperate to win an argument. Or at the very least to convince himself that God was on his side.

He wasn't wrong about contemplation, though. As any angler knows, something happens to the mind while the body is engaged in fishing, a strange marriage of focus and free rein, not entirely unrelated to mindfulness, I imagine. Thoughts wander and you pull them back. Each moment gains its own kind of inner expansiveness.

This contemplative side to angling is, I assume, the main reason the activity has spawned so many books. There's a lot of time to think when you're fishing. A lot of time to wonder what on earth it is you're doing, to consider the ridiculous as well as the sublime. That deep focus is helpful too. It lends itself directly, pragmatically, to writing. The poet Ted Hughes once said that the skills required to concentrate his thoughts on a poem had not been taught to him in school. Instead, he learned them while fishing, his eyes centred on a float, his mind turning circles around that bright tether, that trembling quill, where the real and the imagined meet.

Time, focus, curiosity: these are the essential ingredients of both angling and writing. And of reading, too.

Books about fishing are usually centred around one of two questions: *How* or *Why*. They offer technical advice or elaborate self-justification. Even those that amount to mere fishy tales, accounts of what's been caught and where, are really stories about motivation. A rare few – and *The Compleat Angler* is one – have things to say about both, but for the most part, authors keep these enquiries separate.

This book falls quite comfortably into the latter category. Though it isn't asked directly throughout, that question, *Why*, lies behind almost everything here. Why is it that this activity provides so much pleasure, so much fascination, to so many? Why is it that, of the infinite number of ways I could waste my time, I keep choosing this one? Why is it that, for me, angling can make the world feel bigger, richer and more complex?

I wrote previously that my identity as an angler needed no qualifications, but that doesn't mean that no qualifications can be made. I am, for one thing, a fly fisher primarily, and I cast for brown trout more often than for any other species. I am also, undeniably, an angler of middling talent. I have been fishing for a long time, and am competent within a limited set of circumstances, but beyond those I quickly, sometimes happily, descend into ineptitude.

I have chosen to ask *Why* rather than *How*, therefore, partly out of necessity, because it is the only question I am even moderately qualified to tackle. What little I have to offer by way of technical advice is not really worth writing down, and would probably be best ignored. But *Why* is also the question that matters most to me, the one to which I keep returning, again and again.

I have written this book for two simple reasons. Firstly, angling interests me. It occupies, intrigues and confuses me. When my mind is not doing something else, it is usually drifting towards water, and I am usually content to let it go. This movement, to and from the waterside, is one of the underlying rhythms of my days, and it is echoed here in these pages. This book leapfrogs between locations and times, from my childhood to the present day; but the organizing principle is that rhythm. The chapters alternate between those that are centred around a place and those that are centred around an idea or subject. It is a kind of cast and retrieve, if you like, back and forth, from action to contemplation.

My second reason for writing has been expressed most succinctly by the novelist and angling author, W. D. Wetherell. 'I write about fly fishing,' he explained, in *One River More*, 'because I enjoy writing about delight.' I began this book in the summer of 2020, six months into the Covid-19 pandemic, a time in which delight felt harder to come by and therefore more urgent than ever. Writing it, I turned to what has been the most consistent source of joy and consolation in my life, and I found myself asking, *Why?*

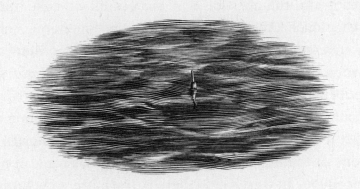

SCALAND WOOD

East Sussex, 1989

ALL ANGLERS HAVE ORIGIN STORIES, a place and time from which their interest, their obsession, springs. Some are dulled by inevitability: the familiar tale of a hobby passed from parent to child. But the best of them are entirely improbable, events that really ought not to have happened. Such stories insist on the rather dizzying idea that, had things gone another way, had this one random moment never come, an entire life might have been different.

The reason these stories are so prevalent, and the reason they carry such weight, is because fishing is not like football; it's not part of the day-to-day background noise of popular culture. Nor is it like tennis, or golf, with high-profile competitive events to attract attention. And though there are similarities between the two pastimes, fishing isn't like birding, either. Whether we choose to notice them or not, birds are a presence in our days (the act of noticing being the first step towards becoming a birder). By contrast, the objects of anglers' attention generally go unseen. To look at fish properly, you really need to hold one in your hand. There is, therefore, something of a paradox – a catch-22, if you'll forgive the pun. To become bewitched by fishing, you have to go fishing.

Which means, usually, that someone else has to take you.

I don't remember a great deal about the man who set it all off, this decades-long fixation. He was known as Paddy, I'm sure of that. But I'm equally sure that it was not his real name. He was a man from Northern Ireland, living in England at the end of the 1980s, and Paddy, back then, was just what people called him.

I remember that he wore a moustache, and that he smoked a pipe. That's how I see him, at least, and I hope that recollection is correct. He was an acquaintance of my parents, but not someone they knew well. It's possible that he and my mother had come to know each other because she was the only other person from Northern Ireland in town. What I know for sure is that on the day he took us fishing – my brother Rory and me, aged seven and eight – Paddy was essentially a stranger, a man with whom we had never spent time before. I have tried to imagine how this came about, this unlikely scenario, but I can't come up with anything that feels entirely satisfactory. I could, of course, ask my mother to tell me how it happened. It's possible she would remember. But sometimes it's better not to contaminate the haze of one's own memories with the awkward air of someone else's.

Whatever the reason, Paddy picked us up on that morning and he drove us through Jarvis Brook, a village on the edge of Crowborough, in East Sussex, where we lived. We arrived at Scaland Wood and found a space at the edge of a little lake, its banks congested by trees. There was just room enough there for Paddy to sit in his folding chair, with Rory and I perched on the ground on either side of him. There was no one else at the lake at all.

I can see that space now, tucked in beneath branches, and the view outwards over the clay-brown water, with a clarity that seems implausible after more than thirty years. What I also see are the lily pads gathered to the left of where we cast, the narrow, orange-tipped float, beneath which our hook and bait were hanging, and the fish we caught: silver roach, with pale red fins, and crucian carp, of burnt-butter yellow. What glittering, enchanting things those fish were, drawn out from beneath that murky surface. Even their very names seemed to carry a kind of magic. *Crucian*: can there be a more sublime word than that?

What I remember more clearly still, though, was a feeling I had never experienced before, a feeling of taut anticipation, of thrilling stillness. Watching that float, waiting for the moment it would dip and disappear, I had the sense that something monumental was happening. For the first time, I seemed to understand that the world held astonishing secrets, and that if I could only spend my time searching for them, I would be happy. That knowledge, that sensation, has never left me.

Both of us, Rory and I, were ecstatic on our return home, and from that day forward I was gripped by a fervent obsession. Fruitless attempts to repeat our success, using bamboo canes, bent pins and string, did nothing to dissuade us, and so, a few months later, my uncle Joseph took me to buy my first proper fishing rod, at an antiques shop just up the road from where we lived. It was a strange building, always dark inside, no matter how bright the day, and there was a courtyard at the back, with clear plastic sheets to separate the indoors from the out. I remember dirt on the floors, and near-chaotic clutter. In a gloomy corner, at one end of the shop, was a barrel with half a dozen rods jumbled inside. I took one of them home. It was old, but certainly not an antique. Made of muddy-brown fibreglass, it was heavy and unwieldy, and I could not have been more delighted.

It's curious that this stuff comes back to me, and so clearly, after all these years. Curious that I should retain such sharp recollection from a time in my life that is otherwise almost gone. Ordinarily, my memory isn't up to much. It is distinctly net-like, in fact, letting loose far more than it carries. Yet I remember fishing. I remember lakes I haven't seen in nearly thirty years. I remember afternoons spent on boats and piers and rocky shores and heather-smothered banks. I remember numberless days in which nothing remarkable happened, except that I was searching for fish. Looking back, my life is illuminated by water.

There is a kind of presence I feel when fishing that is unlike other kinds of presence. Even when my mind wanders, as it does, I am entirely resident within a particular moment and a particular place. And in any day's angling, there are always times – a few minutes, an hour, maybe more – when all attention gathers inside its own instant, when sensation and thought are held right there, right then. When that happens, there is nothing else.

This deep attentiveness to time and place, this undivided presence, is one of the reasons that even uneventful days can be imprinted so profoundly. The details that accumulate in such moments give to them a bulk that outweighs mere drama. What they have, these memories, is a lavish specificity, combined with a quietude that is more profound than almost any other we experience in our lives. The days we spend fishing, as Ted Leeson has written, are 'small stillnesses in the incessancy of the world'. That stillness and specificity endure.

Of course, the passion helps as well. The obsession. The total preoccupation. The turning things over in your mind. The reliving of catches and losses. The endless dreaming. In those first half-dozen years after taking it up, I was fixated by fishing. I trained nearly all of my childhood fervour in that direction. I read about fishing, talked about fishing, thought about fishing, and whenever I could, I *went* fishing.

It's not quite like that now. Such fervour doesn't often

survive one's teens. It simmers down – and that was certainly the case for me. The obsession dimmed to mere enthusiasm, with occasional relapses as the years went by. It happens to most of us, I guess. Youthful passion gets squeezed by the self-consciousness of our teenage years, then squeezed further by the various burdens of adult life. If we're not lucky, it gets snuffed out completely.

Though I never stopped fishing, I do feel the want of that single-minded zeal. Like other things I have lost along the way, it's still there, waiting, when I look back. And when I think about it now, that's part of what fishing is for me: a looking back, a longing, a reaching for unreachable things. It is an active, corporeal nostalgia. Chris Yates has said that 'all anglers are still children', but that's just wishful thinking. What's true, rather, is that angling is an attempt to rekindle something that burned brightest in childhood. It is an attempt – in vain, of course, but irresistible nevertheless – to return to that moment when an angler first found themselves enthralled, that moment when they first were struck by the mystery of what lay beneath the water's surface, and by the desire to uncover and submit to that mystery. Every cast made as an adult is aimed backwards.

Throughout my life I have been trying to retrieve something of that early encounter with wonder, that overwhelming feeling of excitement, of discovery, of possibility, of awe. Every time I pick up a fishing rod, even now, I am trying to go back to Scaland Wood, to experience again the thrill of learning that the world can be coaxed into such glorious disclosure.

A
FLEETING THING

THERE'S A LAKE THAT I think about sometimes: a long, narrow-waisted stretch of water, hugged between mountains, somewhere in the north of Vancouver Island. I've been there only once, aged fourteen, when we visited my mother's Canadian relatives for the first time.

The lake was high up in the hills, a long way from the nearest town, and the only obvious evidence of human habitation that I can recall was the campsite at one end where we stayed for a few days, the three adults sleeping in a campervan, my brother and I in a tent. My mother's cousin also brought her cat along. It spent part of each day wandering fearfully among the trees, and the rest of the time gazing out over the water.

The Canadians were well equipped for life outdoors

(as Canadians are apt to be). In addition to the camper-van and the tent, they had all the barbecue gear you could ever hope for, and a rowing boat, with a tiny outboard engine, so we could get out on the water. For my brother and me, that boat was a wondrous thing. Twisting the throttle, feeling the air strike our faces as we skipped over the ripples, it could hardly have been more exciting. Even the little orange lifejackets, strapped so tight around us we could barely breathe, did not restrict our enjoyment.

We had fishing rods with us on that trip, of course – one each, for my brother and me – and there were trout to be caught. Each evening, they would come to the surface, their rises piercing the stillness. But try as we might, we couldn't catch them. We couldn't catch them from the boat and we couldn't catch them from the shore. I remember one night, Rory and I standing alongside each other, casting into the dusk, our fly lines swishing back and forth as bats flustered over the water. We feared they might mistake our artificial flies for real ones, and we wondered what we'd do if we accidentally hooked one. But we needn't have worried. The bats were no more susceptible to our efforts than the trout. We were both still learning to fly fish back then, and our technique left a lot to be desired. We had few ideas about how to fool these fish, and none of them worked.

It didn't matter, though. Not one bit. We could hardly have been happier. And that happiness derived not just from the freedoms we were allowed there, but from the place itself, which was surely the most beautiful lake I had ever seen. Maybe it still is, if I had to choose.

I'm not sure if beauty is something children think about all that much. It's not really part of how they judge the world. They are sensitive, of course, to the inner urgency of *wonder*, and they develop a recognition of *prettiness* that is at least partly determined by popular culture – and by television, most of all. But a sense of beauty comes more slowly. It builds on both of those perceptions, combining them with something like *taste*, a gradual accumulation of responses to what is seen, which ultimately settle into certainty.

I don't remember having been struck quite so forcefully before that trip, with the clear conviction that a place was beautiful. But it struck me then, and hard. Why? Well, who knows? Perhaps some golden ratio of mountain, sky and water was at play, a formula even my youthful eye could recognize. More likely though, the lake appealed to something already inside me, some yearning I had for wildness, and for landscapes entirely unlike those I had known before. This, together with the knowledge that our stay would be brief, and that we might see this place only once in our lives, gave it an ethereal quality, a perfection granted only to what cannot last. So while the judgement was directed outwards – the *lake* is beautiful – that thought, in truth, said as much about me as it did about the water.

This experience, this certainty, shaped me. In one way or another, every place I've visited since then has been measured against that one. And though it was not a view I could immediately articulate, that trip left me with the peculiar idea that beauty might have something to do with fishing, or that fishing might have something to do with beauty. Nothing in all the years that have passed has persuaded me otherwise.

I took a photograph, just before we packed away our tent. That's what you do when faced with perfection; you try to take a slice of it home. I have it still: a small, square image, of which water makes up the bottom half. Above, two pine-clad slopes, one on either side, like the snouts of glaciers, almost meeting in the middle. Beyond, the sharp-angled outline of a mountain peak, and a wedge of blue-white sky. I dug the picture out of a cardboard box the other day, and was pleased to see it had faded, just a little, the whole image veiled by that haze of age that seems only to prove the distance between then and now.

There is another picture of that weekend, too, a larger one, painted in oil by my mother's cousin. The view on that canvas is almost identical to the one in the photograph: the lake, the hills, the mountain. The difference between hers and mine – other than the medium – is the boat she painted out on the water, and the two little boys within, each in orange lifejackets. In the foreground, surveying the scene, sits a cat.

Like birding, like hiking, like climbing, like wild swimming, the appeal of angling cannot be fully separated from the places in which angling happens. For a particular kind of person, the most beautiful places are those that contain water, and the most beautiful water is that which contains fish. This relationship isn't incidental. While not every angler would put it in these terms – and while some, I suspect, might scoff at the very notion – the pursuit of fish is, at least in part, a pursuit of beauty.

That doesn't mean, of course, that fishing is merely an excuse to look at pretty scenery. It is not just a damp form of sightseeing. What fishing offers, rather, is an immersion in that scenery, an envelopment of a person by a place. It offers beauty not as something to be admired, like a painting, or gawped at in awe, like some Romantic, mist-soaked vista, but as something to be inhabited, to be known, to be experienced.

I have lost count of the number of books I've read in which an author earnestly implores their readers to 'connect' with nature or 'engage' with place, for the sake of their mental health, or the environment, or both. These instructions, though well-meaning, are rarely accompanied by any substantive articulation of what that connection or engagement might actually look like, how it might meaningfully be enacted. Is being outside enough? Should one also learn the names of birds or beetles? If so, how many names does it take? Is it necessary, really, to leap into icy streams to swim?

For me, being in the presence of a place for an extended period of time is when engagement begins to feel tangible. A place reveals itself only gradually. This can happen through repeated visits, through coming to know somewhere, slowly, as one might a person. But it comes most predictably during long stretches of near-silent proximity. As minutes and hours pass, my attention is drawn to what had previously been unnoticed. Those creatures that are disturbed by my arrival may slowly return, accepting my presence or forgetting I am there. Time brings the layers of a place to the light, exposing what cannot be seen in a glance. It is, for the most part, a quiet revelation.

I experience that kind of engagement most often when fishing. For no other reason would I spend six, seven hours in one place, not talking, not looking at my phone, just letting that place *be*, so it's no surprise that I see more, hear more, notice more in those hours than at other times outdoors. It's no surprise that I feel myself becoming acquainted. But fishing offers more than just the *opportunity* for engagement. It also provides a literal connection, a direct line to the natural world. The angler does not just look and listen; the angler interacts. They learn a place through each one of their senses, and can come, through touch, to know the unseen as well as the seen.

The ultimate goal in angling is to connect. It is to have the life of a place surround and absorb you. It is to reach out and to find something reaching back. When that happens – when the hook meets its target and the angler is fastened to the world – 'You become the fish,' as Tracy K. Smith, in her poem 'Astral', has put it. 'Desire tethered to desire.' The whole pursuit culminates in that intense moment of connection, when a place makes known yet another piece of its beauty.

*

The place that I know best, the one in which I have spent most time in my life, and certainly most time fishing, is Shetland: the scattered archipelago at the far north of the British Isles. We moved there from the south of England when I was nine – my mother, my brother and I. It was a year or so after our first ever fishing trip, but I hadn't improved very much in the meantime. I was still, in reality, a complete beginner.

There was an upside and a downside to moving to Shetland, as far as angling was concerned. The downside was that the kinds of fish and fishing to which I had thus far been introduced did not exist. There are no 'coarse' species in the islands, other than eels. There are no carp, no roach, no tench, no perch. So most of what I had learned thus far was useless. But the ease with which it was possible to go fishing more than made up for it. We lived in Lerwick then, just a minute or two's walk from the harbour, and there were countless places around the shore where sea fish could be caught. It wasn't necessary to be accompanied by an adult, either; I was free to fish alone if I wanted, or with my brother, if I had to. And what made things even easier was that, in Shetland, there were lots of people who could help me when I needed it. Some of my new classmates fished; the lodger we had for our first year in the islands fished; our next-door neighbour fished. Where previously angling had seemed an esoteric activity, its practitioners a mysterious fellowship to which I craved admittance, now anglers were ten a penny. So, while coarse fishing would have to wait for summer holidays in England, where my father still lived, there would be no shortage of other options in the meantime.

I fished mainly in the sea to begin with. It was the most accessible place, and the most forgiving of my limited abilities. All I had to do was drop my line from the pier into the water and wait. If I was feeling ambitious, I could cast a metal lure or some feathered hooks. I caught tiny coalfish (which in Shetland we called *sillocks*), flounders (which we called *flukes*), scorpionfish (which we called *pluckers*) and occasionally mackerel (which we called mackerel).

But though I fished at the harbour after school and at weekends, whenever the weather allowed, I was never fully converted to sea angling. Somehow, the ocean felt too large and unknowable to me, and it was always fresh-water that appealed most of all. While I liked the variety of species you could find around the coast, and I tried pretty hard to catch them, from the very beginning of our time in Shetland what I really wanted to catch was trout.

Most anglers have in their heads some kind of hierarchy of fish (though they might not admit that fact to a stranger). This will not be a complete hierarchy, of course, just a partial list: those species about which the angler knows enough to make some kind of value judgement, based on their own priorities, their own prejudices, their own eccentric standards. The species on this list will usually comprise those fish the angler has actually caught or seen first-hand, though it may include others, too: fish they have read about, seen pictures of, or merely imagined.

For some, the size and strength of fish will be the principal criteria on which their judgement is based. Big and brawny is the winning combination. For others, the flattering light of nostalgia, of childhood association, is what makes some species shine. But one measure that nearly always plays a part in such list-making is beauty. The attractiveness or otherwise of fish species is a key part of the affection in which anglers hold them.

I suspect this may be hard to understand for those who only ever encounter haddock in a supermarket, or herring laid out in a fishmonger's window. Stiff, pale-eyed and drying: they can verge, then, on the grotesque. But these are hardly the appropriate settings in which to make an aesthetic judgement. Most animals look better when alive, after all. Seen in their own habitat, fish can be spectacular, as impressive as any bird. Holding themselves in a current, fanning their bodies to remain in place, they are graceful, elegant creatures. And yet, to most people, they are invisible.

It's in the eye of the beholder, of course, as far as ranking species goes. Or, to some degree it is. Take the common carp, for instance, which for many in the UK and Europe is the unrivalled piscine champion. This is a fish with many devoted admirers, some of whom would never dream of chasing any other fish. Yet, while they may be a handsome bronze in colour, a carp's visual appeal is principally about scale. They can be grand and impressive, if you like that sort of thing. But if you don't, they are merely corpulent, with a dim-witted expression quite at odds with their reputation for guile. I find myself, these days, in the latter camp.

I am more sympathetic when it comes to the carp's distant, smaller cousins: the dace, the rudd, the roach. I am also fond of the tench, which is a rare, golden green in colour, and which, sometimes, can seem almost to glow. But my own shortlist of the prettiest fish – narrowing it down, for now, to those in British waters, fresh and salt – would not include any of these species. Instead, I would choose the perch, the grayling, the mackerel and the cuckoo wrasse. And above all others, I would choose the trout.

By 'trout', here, I mean the brown trout in particular. Though really, if I can widen my choice, I mean the whole Salmoninae subfamily, and the freshwater species especially. I am not quite as awed by salmon as some anglers seem to be, but the trout and the chars are unsurpassable: beautiful, I think, beyond compare.

My pocket-sized copy of *The Observer's Book of Freshwater Fishes*, an otherwise moderate and even-handed guide, makes this startlingly unscientific assertion in its chapter on *Salmo trutta*: 'If there can be said to be such a thing as the "perfect fish" then that fish is the Trout.' In fact, there is something about this particular fish, or this family of fishes, that invites extravagant praise. There is something about their vivid, speckled elegance that demands superlatives. They are, as the angling writer John Gierach once observed, 'a hell of a lot prettier than they need to be'.

One of the most remarkable things about these fish – a fact that only emphasizes their extraordinary beauty – is their diversity, the extreme variation in size, appearance and behaviour that can be found within a single species. A brown trout, for instance, may be as pale as a pilchard or as dark as peaty water. It may be egg-yolk yellow or olive green. It may hold hints of blue and orange. The constellation of spots on its flanks will be unique to each individual, some combination of black and scarlet, large and small, and each mark may be circled in silver. Trout are one of those animals that stretch and warp the very idea of species, the borders we humans draw between one creature and another. Still today, there is no consensus on how many types of trout actually exist.

That same *Book of Freshwater Fishes*, first published in 1941, names eleven species of native trout in Britain and Ireland, whereas today biologists recognize only two: the brown trout, *Salmo trutta*, and the Gillaroo, *Salmo stomachicus* (the latter of which is not universally acknowledged as separate from the former). A single lake may contain several visually and genetically distinct groups of trout, all of which sit under that one enormous umbrella: *Salmo trutta*. Then, too, there are the sea trout, which spend most of their lives in saltwater, and which look quite different from brown trout, but, taxonomically speaking, are the very same fish. And let's not even start on the chars, of which there may be just one species native to all of Europe, or else fifteen in the British Isles alone, depending on whom you ask. As for the rest of the world, well, frankly, it's anyone's guess.

If part of the appeal of coarse fishing and sea fishing is the variety of species one may catch, that variety is not lost by focusing only on trout. I have caught many hundreds in my time, and every single one of them was different. They are, I think, magnificent creatures, as beautiful a thing as exists on this earth. As beautiful as hummingbirds, as cherry blossoms, as swallowtail butterflies. When I chose, early on, to pursue trout, this magnificence was one of the rewards.

Trout thrive in clean, cold water. They thrive in high-country brooks, chalk streams, alpine lakes and clear, limestone lochs. They thrive in places that tend towards the picturesque, and their presence implies a splendour that goes well beyond the aesthetic. The existence of trout relies upon the health of the water, the health of an entire ecosystem. It relies upon an abundance of insects, which in turn relies upon and sustains an immense network of other living things, of microorganisms, plants, birds, amphibians. Trout are proof of life, in other words. They are the vitality of a habitat, embodied.

There are literally hundreds of lochs spread out across the islands of Shetland, and nearly all of those lochs contain trout. It is a perfect place for them – clean and cold – and a perfect place, too, for the budding trout angler.

I started fishing for them the easy, unlovely way, with a worm and a float. And not the slender, elegant floats I knew from coarse fishing, either. Those were too light to be cast any meaningful distance, and too frail to stand up to the near-constant wind in the islands. No, the necessary tool for this job was a 'bubble float', a hollow sphere of thick, fluorescent plastic, which could be half-filled with water to give it weight. Get the balance right between water and air, and you could hurl those things halfway across a loch and still not lose sight of them. They were sturdy and practical, and as ugly as a shaved cat.

I don't remember when or why exactly I decided to try a different technique. It might have been a magazine that did it – nobody used bubble floats in *Trout and Salmon*. Or else it might have been the fact that few grown-ups I saw fishing were doing what I was doing. Instead, most of the trout anglers I spotted in Shetland were fly fishing, waving rods around like magic wands, without floats or worms to weigh them down. From afar, I was converted, and by the time I was thirteen, or thereabouts, I was doing my best to emulate those other anglers.

And my best? Well, for a long time, it wasn't good enough.

Activities that lean towards grace and artistry will, in the hands of the unskilled, expose the opposite qualities. There are few things more undignified or ridiculous than someone learning to cast with a fly rod. Particularly someone who is teaching themselves from a book, rather than being taught in person. Absolutely nothing I had learned before then had provided me with the skills that fly fishing demanded – skills of timing, balance, and a sensitivity to motion that is unconnected to anything else in angling. Or, indeed, anything else in life. Get it right, and something quite astounding happens. Get it wrong, and your hook won't even end up in the water.

It amazes me now that I persisted, flailing around, tangling myself in fly line, hooks piercing my clothing and my skin, catching nothing whatsoever for month after month, and yet not giving up. Where did that persistence come from? Certainly, I couldn't muster it these days. I couldn't put myself through that kind of frustration and humiliation again. I would at least find someone else to show me what to do, to point out my mistakes and to help me correct them. But back then, I just kept flailing. And thank goodness for that!

'The real truth about fly-fishing,' wrote John Gierach, is that 'it is beautiful beyond description in almost every way, and when a certain kind of person is confronted with a certain kind of beauty, they are either saved or ruined for life, or a little of both.' Fly fishers have a bad reputation for claiming the superiority of their tactics over those of other anglers – technical superiority, moral superiority – and for the most part those claims are bunk. But in this one way, in pure aesthetic terms, there is simply no competition.

Anyone who doubts the visual appeal of fly fishing should probably begin their education by watching Robert Redford's 1992 film, *A River Runs Through It*. In fact, that's exactly where many fly fishers did begin. The release of that film, which was based on Norman Maclean's autobiographical novella of the same name, and which starred a young Brad Pitt, led to an explosion of interest in the sport. Within two years of its release, the American fly-fishing industry had more than doubled in size. Many thousands of people saw the gorgeous Montana landscape in which it was set, bathed in a syrupy light; they saw the balletic fly casting of the actors (or their body doubles) carving intricate loops of line through the air. They saw it all, and they thought, *I want to do that*. When I watched it on television, clumsy and fumbling as I still was, aged fourteen, I thought the very same thing.

A River Runs Through It is a beautiful film, and the book on which it is based contains, to my mind, some of the most exquisite sentences in the English language. But both film and book are, moreover, *about* beauty: the pursuit of it and the loss of it. The word 'beautiful' recurs again and again throughout, together, often, with the word 'grace'. The narrator's father, John Maclean, a Scots Presbyterian minister in Missoula, Montana, views fly fishing as a means of 'picking up God's rhythms', and the inordinate difficulty of learning to cast a fly rod well as proof of that significance. 'To him, all good things – trout as well as eternal salvation – come by grace and grace comes by art and art does not come easy.'

Trout, according to the Reverend John Maclean, are the heavenly reward for fishing well. But that faithful logic is tested, painfully, by the narrator's brother, Paul. Between the three of them – the two brothers and their father – it is Paul who is the truly great fisherman. He is the one who can stop people in their tracks, the gossamer spray from his fly line conjuring 'a halo of himself', the air above the river 'iridescent with the arched sides of a great Rainbow'. As he casts, 'The canyon was glorified by rhythms and colors.'

But Paul himself cannot be saved. He is killed, violently, while still a young man, and Norman and his father are forever haunted by that loss. In one of the few conversations they ever have about Paul after his death, Norman insists that he has nothing left to say about his brother:

> 'I've told you all I know. If you push me far enough, all I really know is that he was a fine fisherman.'
>
> 'You know more than that,' my father said. 'He was beautiful.'
>
> 'Yes,' I said, 'he was beautiful. He should have been – you taught him.'

Writing a story, like taking a photograph or painting a picture, is a way of trying to capture and possess beauty, to hold on to what cannot, in fact, be held. The best that can be hoped for is the creation of another kind of beauty altogether, a more permanent, fabricated kind. The kind that shimmers through Norman Maclean's sentences. The kind that was not his brother's at all, but his own.

Fishing, too, is a way of trying to capture what is beautiful, though the angler cannot even pretend to possess that beauty. Not for more than a moment. A fish, caught, is a fleeting thing. It can be killed or returned to the water, but either way it is lost, preserved only in the memory. The best you can do, really, is to cast again.

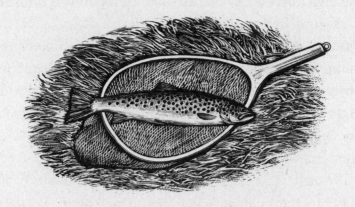

THE BACK
OF RONAS HILL

Shetland, 2020

FROM WHERE WE STOOD, IT was just a white speck on the hillside, the slightest interruption to the heather, moss and pink granite. With the naked eye, I could hardly pick it out at all, but my brother Rory, with binoculars, insisted it was worth a closer look. So we trudged upwards over boggy ground, hop-stepping, splashing, through a peat-black burn, banks spotted with flowering sundews, then higher, to a hummock of tufted grass where we paused and looked again.

The speck was now a shape, a living thing for sure, and the list of what that thing might be was short. We passed the binoculars between us then continued, more cautiously this time, not wanting to cause a disturbance. But there was no cover here to hide us. As the slope steepened, finally, we stopped, a couple of hundred metres from where the shape was perched among the rocks. Even without the glasses there was no longer any doubt. With them, we could see it watching us: a snowy owl, a male, the kind of perfect white that seems impossible, imagined.

The bird lifted, nervous of our proximity, and its broad wings opened, silent, to the sky. As it flew, a pair of Arctic skuas rose, shrieking, and took chase, and a single bonxie – a great skua, mottled brown and enormous – did the same. The owl ignored its attackers and settled near the top of the closest ridge, shimmying back into position, still watching us. We let it be, walked a few dozen metres down the hill, then turned to look again. It was nowhere to be seen.

This was the northern slope of Ronas Hill, the highest point in the Shetland Islands. At just 450 metres, it is some way short of a mountain, but it is an imposing presence nonetheless, rising as it does from near vertical sea cliffs on its southern and western sides. With its steep flanks of pink-studded tundra, it is a place that seems to belong more to the Arctic than to the British Isles. The owl, though not a usual resident, only amplified that feeling.

While a pair of binoculars is nearly always around Rory's neck, he and I were not there to look at birds. We were there to fish. The plateau of bog and moor and granite that lies north of this hill holds some of the very best fishing in Shetland, and some of the most appealingly named lochs as well. Clubbi Shuns, Many Crooks, Maadle Swankie: these are among the ones that can be found on maps. Others, like the Loch of the Grey Yowe, are part of an oral geography, a map held in memory alone.

What is most striking about this place, though, at least to an angler, is just how many lochs and lochans there are. On paper you can see what, from the ground, is often obscured: there is water everywhere. In a stretch of roughly seven square miles – all of it far from any paved road – there are several dozen lochs large enough to be worth fishing. And almost any of them may hold trout. There can be few places in this country where one could fish so many pieces of water, on foot, in a single day.

But this is a place in which it is easy to get lost. In low light or in fog, one loch can look much like another. There are few visible landmarks with which to guide yourself – no trees, no paths, no man-made structures – and in the days before our phones held maps and GPS, a compass was a necessary part of any angler's equipment here. This may be only a small corner of an island, but it's a place that seems bigger underfoot. Beside a hill that feels like a mountain, this is a plateau that feels like a world of its own.

Rory and I began our day in Swaabie Water, the closest loch to where we'd parked, at the summit of Collafirth, Ronas Hill's shorter neighbour. After the thrill of the owl, the fishing began rather quietly: a few half-hearted splashes at the flies, a few palm-sized trout. There are bigger ones in here, certainly, but a combination of wind and weed made much of the loch unfishable. So we decided to move on.

To the north and west, nearer to the ocean, is Sandy

Water. Large and brilliantly clear, it is among the most scenic of these lochs, and for me it has always been a highlight of any day up here. My first few casts, into a deep bay on the southern shore, again brought a splash, and an eight-inch fish of bright silver came reluctantly to the net. I slipped it back and felt it wriggle from my hand, an electric jolt of refound freedom.

By now, rain clouds were squalling over the western shoulder of Ronas Hill, and several times a curtain of mist rolled down the slopes and threatened to engulf the plateau. Down it came, then back, as though it couldn't quite make up its mind. A brisk wind scurried across the water, carrying with it a few light-coloured caddisflies (known as sedges), but little other insect life was visible. That didn't discourage the fish, though, and the splashes kept coming. Then, as I was walking westward, with the line dragging behind me, a better fish took, no more than a foot out from the bank. It dived immediately and bent the rod, thrashing its head in frustration. The strength of it took me by surprise, and my focus at once was fastened to that creature, each shake of its body transmitted to my wrist. It was a few minutes before I could convince it to come in, and when it did, I could hardly believe its size. Not much bigger than three-quarters of a pound, it seemed to be built of muscle and mouth and nothing more. It was perfect, and I slipped it back gratefully.

We moved again, because that's what you do out here. Fishing thoroughly, methodically, means missing out, since there are so many lochs to explore; and for most anglers who visit this place, variety takes precedence.

Instead of taking the time to figure things out, to learn one loch, they prospect: walk and cast, walk and cast. They look for the trout that are willing to take, rather than trying to convince the more cautious. A bushy imitation sedge is ideal for this purpose – some highly buoyant combination of deer hair and fur. Even on days like this one, when few fish are rising, there are nearly always some willing to investigate a big fly making a commotion on the surface.

We headed north, to the Loch of the Hog-holm. At least, I think that's where we were. There are three lochs close together around there, and I forget which is which. But in one of them I found another nice trout around ten ounces, which embarked on such elaborate acrobatics that, once it was unhooked, I had to stop, attempt to untangle, then cut and replace my tippet (the thinnest part of the line, to which the flies are attached). I did it slowly. This, I think, is another of the most picturesque spots, with great wedges of pink granite stacked steeply on two sides of the loch. From certain points, looking north, you can see the sheer red cliffs of Lang Clodie Wick, where streams plummet nearly a hundred metres from the plateau to the sea. I tied my knots, looked around, watched Rory casting on the opposite bank, then we made another move.

It's hard to say exactly where we went from there. Partly because most of the lochs we visited have no names that I'm aware of, and partly because I wasn't in control of navigation. 'This way,' Rory would say, looking up from the map on his phone. 'Just over that ridge,' he'd point, and I'd follow. We fished more or less at random, with only a vague deadline ahead of us, and a long walk back to the car to keep in mind. Several times, something like sunshine would lighten the grey sky, and the breeze lost its bitter edge. Then, just as quickly, that roll of mist would creep like a glacier back over the hill, and a thin drizzle would surround us, threatening to thicken into rain.

In a loch no bigger than an acre I spooked a trout at the bank as I approached. It looked a better fish than those we'd caught so far, and I cursed myself for not taking more care. I knelt down, setting the flies close in on one side of me, then the other, but of course the chance had gone. Five minutes passed, then a couple more. My cautious stance was abandoned, and I cast again, towards the middle of the loch. I took a few steps to the right, pulling the line haphazardly behind me. And then a fish was on. I didn't see it take. I wasn't watching. But I heard it, and I felt the rod bend over.

One of the most exciting things about this place is the sheer diversity of these waters, and of what they contain. Some lochs are chock-full of tiny trout, which hurl themselves like piranhas at almost any fly they see. Others, though, may hold much larger fish. Not knowing what lies within, as you first cast your fly, is part of the appeal. Especially because, up here, big fish may be in unexpected places.

The trout of this plateau are isolated. They are the descendants of those trout that were stranded here after the last ice age, as the cliffs on the western edge eroded, leaving them exiled from the sea. I doubt whether any of these lochs have ever been stocked with fish from else-where. But that doesn't mean that stocking does not go on. After all, there are lochs up here where the opportunities for trout to breed are limited or non-existent: no significant burns in or out, no gravel beds. Which means that some, by rights, should be empty. But local anglers don't always leave them that way. A trout of half a pound caught in one loch can very easily be released into another, a few hundred yards away. And if competition there is limited or non-existent, that trout won't stay half a pound for long. It will grow rapidly. I've seen big fish caught here in lochans that are not much more than puddles.

The trout I'd hooked was not enormous, but it was certainly decent. It didn't fight like the others, didn't make a spectacle of itself, but I could feel the weight of it, the certainty of its resistance. I pulled and it pulled back. I reeled in and it took some line. The resistance weakened quickly, though, and I felt it turn towards me, ready to come in. And then it stopped. I pulled harder, but it stayed put. I thought for a moment that I'd underestimated the fish, that it was bigger than I'd first imagined. But then I understood. The trout was hooked on the top fly, the scruffy sedge, and as it came into shallow water, the second fly, trailing beneath, had snagged on a rock. It was stuck fast.

I lifted the rod high, and the fish lifted too. Its head rose from the water, as though pegged to a washing line. I eased up a little, let it swim, hoping pressure from another direction might extract the other fly. But the fish couldn't go far. It was tethered from both sides, well out of reach of where my welly boots could take me.

By now, Rory was standing beside me, waiting to see what would happen. He offered his advice. There were two options, he said, as far as he could see. Either I let the line go slack and hope the trout made a run for it, freeing itself from the bottom in the process, or else I take off my boots and my socks and wade. I considered option one, as the drier and therefore more appealing of the two. But with barbless hooks I would almost certainly lose the fish that way, even if I managed to retrieve my flies. And I really didn't want to lose the fish. So I handed Rory the rod.

The water was cold, but not quite so cold as I'd feared. With my jeans rolled up around my knees, I stepped in, felt my bare toes clench against the slippery stones. I moved carefully, edging forward with the net stretched out in front of me. Sharp pebbles dug into my feet, and I tried not to flinch and topple over in the process. The trout waited, and may even have been relieved when I finally slipped the net beneath it. I tugged at the line to free the tail fly and it snapped, immediately. I turned and waded back to the shore.

The trout was worth the wet jeans, puckered skin and sore toes. Leopard-spotted across its back, with a flank and belly the colour of pumpkin flesh, the fish was a pound and a half, maybe slightly more. Not enormous, certainly, but stunning nonetheless. It was also tired, understandably, after its protracted time on the hook, so I got it back in the water, held it steady till its strength returned, then watched it swim eagerly away.

We were heading back in the general direction of the

car, not ready to give up yet, but knowing the clock was ticking. There are several ways to reach the lochs out here, and each of them requires a long walk, either from a track to the north, from the main road to the east, or from the top of Collafirth Hill to the south. Given time restrictions, where you park will decide which lochs you fish. Most often, I've visited those in the north-central part of the plateau, so it was good to explore down here in the south. We fished eight or nine altogether in our shortish day, and three of them I had never visited before – had never even known were there.

The ground for the most part was damp. Tramping between one place and another, we stepped between peaty pools and gravel-strewn burns. The earth squelched beneath our feet. Everywhere, among the short stiff grasses, were little golden spires of bog asphodel, yellow heart-petalled tormentil, and the tight pink bells of blossoming heather. Bog cotton was strewn across the landscape, too, as though scraps of wool had been tossed willy-nilly to the wind. And then, in a soggy hollow, between steep granite ridges, Rory stopped, his foot frozen in mid-air. He took a step back and leaned down.

'Bog orchid!' he exclaimed, seeming hardly able to believe it. I knelt beside him to look.

These scarce little flowers had been recorded previously in only half a dozen locations in Shetland, and this was not one of them. But here they were: three in total, that we could find. Anaemic-looking things – pale green with just the merest hint of yellow, and standing no more than a few centimetres from the ground – the fact Rory had seen them at all seemed to me no less impressive than the plants themselves.

So much of what we saw and heard there at the back of Ronas Hill seemed diminutive. Those flowers, crouching in the peat; the merlin that screeched low, late morning, pursued by skuas; the plaintive mewing of nervous golden plovers; and even several of the lochs themselves, hardly large enough to be labelled lochs at all. And yet, held within a certain kind of attention, of noticing, such things expand. Like the speck of white that became an owl, they grow bigger. Angling, I think, necessitates that kind of attention. It is part of what we do when we fish. Attention to the way the wind moves across a piece of water; to the insects that skitter on its surface or that scuttle beneath its rocks; attention to the shadows and the faint ripples of the fish within. Angling magnifies. It brings the world closer.

But perhaps, too, there are certain places that contain their own kind of expansion, where measurement in miles or metres tells you nothing of how far you've gone or how far is left to go. Such places seem to possess an inner elastic. They widen in response to our presence, and are bigger, somehow, than themselves. This, I think, is one such place.

We walked back to the car in the early evening, after one last loch and one last fish. Heading south and east from there, the summit of Collafirth Hill, where the car was parked, seemed to grow no closer from one step to the next.

THE
IMITATION OF LIFE

IT TOOK A PANDEMIC TO get me tying flies again. Three months in which fishing was not allowed, and all outdoor activities were restricted. The rules imposed in that spring of 2020 led to a geographical shrinking of people's lives, but at the same time it pushed me – and I'm certain many others – towards different sources of pleasure and of hope. Some people noticed the wildlife in their garden or local park for the very first time. They heard the birds singing, amplified by the absence of traffic and aeroplanes. Some people may have purchased binoculars, in order to see the world up close. Others took up gardening, to make their surroundings more beautiful. Me, I bought some hooks, some thread and some feathers.

Tying flies wasn't exactly a new thing for me. It was more of an old thing, long since abandoned. I first learned to tie when I was still in my teens, under the patient instruction of older members of the Shetland Anglers Association. On Tuesday evenings, in the winter, we would gather at the association's clubhouse in Lerwick, and I'd watch, listen, and do my best to repeat what I'd been shown. I had a cheap kit, with basic tools and basic materials, most of which were entirely useless for my purposes: turkey feathers dyed in gaudy hues and hanks of fluorescent yarn were not much needed for traditional loch flies. But I was endowed, then, with an overabundance of enthusiasm, and my fly box filled with ghastly patterns that never once saw the water.

Like many teenage pursuits, however – skateboarding, for instance, and knock-door-run – it didn't last. At some point I put all those materials in a box and closed the lid. Once in a while I would bring them out again, when necessity and frugality demanded. But I'd lost my passion, and what skills I had before were always limited. I'd tie a few, get bored, then back it all would go, into the cupboard for another five years. Then ten. Later, in my thirties, I gave away the box to a friend, more competent and persistent than me. From then on, I thought, when I needed some flies, I would buy them.

So when I sat down to order again the tools of the trade – a vice to grip the hooks, a bobbin holder for dispensing thread, and hackle pliers to hold feathers, as well as a selection of wire, fur and other assorted materials – I was surprised by my own decision, by the eagerness that had revived without warning. These were strange times, I told myself, and strange times insist on change. I browsed for hours online, imagining what I might make, and gathering what I would need in my virtual shopping basket. Then, after a momentary pause, I pressed the button: Buy.

There is something undeniably appealing about the beginning-to-end possibilities of fly fishing, whereby an angler can get involved not only in the wet part of the process, the casting and the catching, but also in the dry: the making of those objects of deception on which everything else depends. I can think of few other hobbies, if any, in which participants habitually manufacture a crucial part of their apparatus. (I like to imagine badminton players impaling goose feathers into cork before a match, but I suspect, regrettably, that they do not.)

A fly, though, is not just an item of equipment or a piece of tackle. It is not like a rod or a reel. It is much more than that. It is the crux of fly fishing, where what is crafted by human hands meets the object of our intentions. It is the tiny concocted thing in which our aspirations are invested. It is the sharpened question mark we affix to the end of our lines, the point in which virtually all of the mystery in this whole mysterious business of fishing is concentrated. And not just one kind of mystery, either.

The biggest source of bafflement for newcomers to fly fishing – other than how one actually casts, of course – are flies themselves. Visit any tackle shop and you'll find hundreds of the things, maybe thousands. There are flies for salmon, for brown trout, for rainbow trout; flies for still water and running water; flies for every season, and for every possible condition. There are flies that look precisely like insects or little fish; there are flies that look like nothing else on earth. So where does one begin with all of this? How does one know what to buy, and what to tie on your line?

Growing up in Shetland, most anglers that I knew fished with traditional wet fly patterns. They had tails of golden pheasant or of wool, those flies; their bodies were built from thread or seal's fur, or from barbs of peacock feather wrapped around; they had hackles of black or brown or claret; some had wings, some tufts of blue jay underneath; most had wire or thin tinsel coiled in loops over the body. They were Black Pennells, Zulus and Ke-Hes, Bibios, Invictas and Butchers: names that said next to nothing about the patterns themselves, and yet which seemed to carry tremendous, evocative weight nonetheless. They were beautiful, I thought, in some hard-to-pin-down way. They were dapper, mostly muted in their colours, beyond a few flashes of scarlet, and were built to a formula, or a series of formulae, which made them feel familiar. They were comforting, too, for a beginner; their very longevity instilled a certain confidence, even when my own successes were minimal. That knowledge of others' past catches was sometimes all the faith I could muster.

I knew from reading fishing magazines that there were many other patterns out there – bigger flies, smaller flies, more brightly coloured flies, more lifelike or imitative flies – and I looked at pictures of them with something like wonder, and something like worry. Was I missing out, I thought, as I turned those glossy pages? Was I limiting my chances by sticking to what I knew? There were local anglers who were more adventurous than me, who were not just looking at those pictures but were learning from them, tying and trying new things, leaving behind those traditional patterns on which I relied. But it takes a certain conviction in one's own abilities in order to experiment, and for a long time, and with good reason, my conviction was limited. I didn't catch many trout in my first few years as a fly fisher, even on patterns that I knew ought to work. So how on earth could I be bold enough to abandon them? My boldness was stunted by my ineptitude – by my poor casting, my lack of knowledge, and my random, slapdash approach to the whole business.

But there was something else, too, a feeling that niggled in a way that now is hard to credit. It was the sense that all these other flies – the ones I saw in magazines, or read about in books – were made for other places, and that their very foreignness to Shetland would doom them, there, to failure. Back then, I probably assumed that most of the flies I knew about, the ones I used and tried to tie, had been invented in the islands, or at least with island trout in mind. They seemed so much at home in that place, I would have struggled to believe just how far some of them had travelled; that they'd been invented by anglers from across Britain, Ireland and beyond, would probably never have occurred to me. And though I was wrong about that, though my narrow notion of the localness of wet fly patterns was mistaken, I wasn't *entirely* wrong. For while the internet, with its limitless instruction and retail, all untethered from place, has accelerated a process of levelling out that has long been under way, the traditions of fly tying and selection were once – and to some degree still remain – partly regional.

In many senses, fly fishing around the world is a fairly homogenous activity. Like all sports and hobbies, there are rules and customs that are universal. There are global brands, aiming their wares at anglers worldwide. Variations in the way people fish are largely about mechanics; different tackle and techniques are just different ways of getting a hook in front of a fish. But flies are not like that. Flies reflect a multitude of national and regional traditions. They carry origin stories and mythologies. They represent practical, philosophical and social divisions. They are cultural artefacts, each and every one of them.

Consider the spiders, for instance, a family of patterns that originated in the north of England and southern Scotland at least two hundred years ago. Some of these flies are still used widely, while others, these days, are rarely seen. What distinguishes them is the simplicity of their design and the vernacular nature of their materials. In construction, most are little more than a thin layer of thread, silk or fur along the length of the hook, with a sparse feather, known as a hackle, wrapped like a collar around the front. The names of these flies often reflect this simplicity, combining the bird from which the hackle is taken with the colour of the body: the Partridge and Orange, for example, and the Snipe and Purple. Whereas most flies are named by, or occasionally after, the person who invented them, the spider patterns, like traditional folk songs, seem like geographical rather than individual creations. The oldest of them were made exclusively from birds and animals that could be found in the regions where the anglers lived: moorhen, woodcock, fieldfare, snipe, starling, partridge, mole and hare. This meant that almost anyone could tie them. They were accessible, egalitarian patterns, grounded in place.

Consider also the nineteenth-century vogue for 'fully dressed' Atlantic salmon flies, which were first developed in Ireland, but which became so pervasive in Scotland as the century progressed that most older, local patterns were displaced entirely. These newfangled flies were gaudy things, so outlandish in colour and complexity that they seem, to me at least, more ridiculous than beautiful, like a Royal Ascot hat. The 'fully dressed' patterns were bouquets of brightly dyed feathers from British species, such as swans and ducks, together with a host of other, more exotic materials: ostrich, jungle cock, Indian crow, Lady Amherst's pheasant, blue macaw. These were not just new feathers for tying flies, they were the avian spoils of empire. And while the inventors of such patterns would sometimes offer an elaborate justification for each extraordinary element of their flies, the essential purpose of all was to be *impressive* – not to fish, necessarily, but to people. The intricate, multi-layered wings, the garish cheeks and horns, the whole preposterous get-up:

it was all about showing off. Only the very skilled could tie them, and only the wealthy could afford them. In a century in which angling became more accessible for many in Britain, with the rapid growth of the railways, other barriers were being simultaneously erected, making salmon fishing a pastime that was out of reach for most people. These flies were one such barrier.

Traditions are funny things, sometimes evolving, sometimes standing still, sometimes splitting and diverging, sometimes hardening into dogma. In the history of fly tying, change has often come slowly, and has been met, on occasion, with stubborn resistance. Most fly tiers have worked within the confines of convention. They have tweaked old patterns, added new materials, altered colours; they have tried doing things a little differently, just to see how they work. But the limits of innovation were often decided in advance. Custom dictated what was possible or desirable, and just as crucially what was not. One tradition might be forced to adapt, or else be pushed aside by another from elsewhere (as with the rather drab Scottish salmon flies that were swept away by the 'fully dressed' fad), but conventions could at times be remarkably inflexible. And none were more so than those of the dry fly anglers of southern England, who rose to prominence in the late nineteenth century. Theirs was at first a purely practical solution to a problem all anglers would at one time have faced, but it became, in time, a strict and obstinate ideology that claimed itself to be not just more successful than other fishing methods, but also ethically superior.

The problem was this: trout sometimes feed on insects at the surface of the water, ignoring other sources of food. The solution: tie flies that will float, thus imitating those insects. This solution was made easier with the introduction of water-repellant substances that, when applied to the body or wings of a fly, would hold it on the surface for longer. Dry fly fishing, as this method came to be known, grew quickly in popularity, and with good reason. Dry flies caught fish. But for some of its pioneers and proponents, this was not just an alternative to wet fly fishing, it had entirely superseded that method. And when, in the early twentieth century, another new technique was developed, imitating underwater nymphs, the response was fierce. Fishing with nymphs, argued the dry fly purists, was a fundamentally unsporting activity that should not be allowed on the hallowed chalk streams of England. How much of this attitude was born of snobbery – wet flies were seen as a northern method, and therefore, by some in the south, as inferior – and how much from plain old cultural conservatism, is not clear. Either way, it was bonkers. Yet, while nymphs are these days fished with great success on rivers and lakes all over the world, there are still corners of England where only the dry fly is allowed.

To that first-time angler in the tackle shop, gazing in bafflement at the trays of flies in front of them, none of this tradition, this change or this controversy will be apparent. None of what has gone before will be visible. In the shop, as online, everything is evened out. There will be wet flies for sale; there will be dry flies and nymphs; there will be streamers and goldheads and buzzers and blobs. There may even be *kebari*, the traditional Japanese flies – simple in design, often with front-facing hackles – that are now gaining some popularity in the West. That first-time angler will likely be unconcerned by all of this history, if they're aware of it at all. For them, the only important question when it comes to choosing and tying a fly is the obvious one: does it catch fish? The problem, for almost any pattern you can think of, is that the answer to this question is, well, *sometimes*.

When the fly-tying tools and materials that I had ordered in my mid-pandemic shopping spree arrived at the house, I unpacked everything and laid it all out on the table. I decided immediately that I would start again, go right back to the beginning. My fly box – which I'd made in woodworking class, in high school, twenty-five years before – was looking very tatty. Those flies I fished with most often were frayed and flecked with rust, while those that were still pristine were the ones I never used. I took the whole lot out, tossed them in a jar and closed the lid. I would tie only what I needed, I decided. I would restock the box with flies that I would use, flies that I would *enjoy* using. So what, then, would those be?

I began with a few old favourites: some of the patterns I've been using since my teens, and for which my affection hasn't waned. Though most of my fishing is done away from Shetland these days, a small number of those traditional wet flies still feel like good company, as do one or two of the most simple nymph patterns, which are rarely off my line. I've caught a lot of fish with them over the years. But of course, I've caught a lot of fish with them precisely because they're rarely off my line. And the same goes for all of these old favourites. The ones I tie on are the ones I catch fish with, and the ones I never use don't catch me anything. How could it be any other way? I like the flies that catch me fish and so I tie them on and so I catch fish with them and so I like them. Etcetera, etcetera. It is a loop of logic with no meaningful entrance or exit, no way to explain my reasoning to someone else. It is a matter of taste, hardened into habit.

This reliance on habit, and the whims of taste, might surprise the newcomer to fly fishing. After all, everything they are likely to read on the subject – the books, the websites, the magazines, the forums – will talk in terms of certainty, in terms of *learning* and of *knowing* what catches fish, where, when and why. That newcomer would be forgiven for imagining that an almost mystical degree of insight into the desires and behaviour of trout is attainable, if only they keep reading. If only they pay attention.

That bullshit is old.

In *A Treatyse of Fysshynge wyth an Angle*, published in 1496 and the first such work in English, the author gave basic dressings for twelve fly patterns, arranged by month. Izaak Walton, who was not much of a fly fisher, it's said, gave the same list in *The Compleat Angler*, just over 150 years later. But by 1676, when the second part of that book was written and added by Charles Cotton, things were getting much more complicated. Cotton described sixty-five flies in total, for use throughout the year. His instructions at times were ludicrously precise (one pattern demanded hair taken from 'the black spot of a hog's ear'), and at other times hopelessly ambiguous (the flies, he wrote, were 'some for one water and one sky, and some for another; and, according to the change in those, we alter their size and colour'). On occasion, he managed to be both precise and ambiguous in a single sentence ('From the sixth of this month [April] to the tenth, we also have a fly called the Violet-fly, made of a dark violet stuff'). Despite all the detail he provided, Cotton did acknowledge that his flies, designed principally for use on the River Dove in the Peak District, might 'do you not great service in your southern rivers'. In fact, he admitted, a friend of his in London, furnished with some of these patterns, 'never did any great feats with them' at all.

Here then, familiar after almost 350 years, is that tone one still encounters in nearly every fly-fishing publication today, online and in print. It is a tone of elaborate confidence, armoured with caveats. It's a tone that demonstrates great expertise on the writer's side, while putting any blame for failure on to the reader.

What much of this advice boils down to – from the *Treatyse* and *The Compleat Angler* all the way to the latest issue of an angling magazine – is the same basic instruction: artificial flies intended to catch trout or grayling should imitate the things that these fish eat. Know what the fish are eating, and you will know what fly to use.

Stated like this, the advice sounds simple, unarguable. It sounds like a practical place to begin for the tier or the buyer of flies. But in fact, 'imitate fish food' is not a command one can follow without question. It offers, rather, a whole spectrum of possible options. At one end of that spectrum are the precise imitative patterns that Charles Cotton might have produced, if the tools and materials available to him in the seventeenth century had allowed it. As the traditional dry fly fishers like to counsel, one should aim to 'match the hatch' (though, of course, much of a fish's diet is not 'hatching' at all, but swimming or crawling or drifting), and many fly tiers work hard to create exact replicas of individual species of insect – *Ephemera danica*, the 'green drake', for instance, or *Rhithrogena germanica*, the 'March Brown' mayfly. This is undoubtedly a serious skill, and one worthy of admiration. The colour, size, shape and posture of the wings, the segmentation of the abdomen, the length of the tail: absolutely everything is taken into account and copied, with materials both natural and man-made. It won't be long, I suppose, before almost any insect can be recreated perfectly with a 3D-printer, ready to be fixed to a hook – if that's what you desire.

Another possible approach to imitation, though, is rather looser and more impressionistic. Flies that impersonate a family or genera of insects are common, and undoubtedly successful. Examples include caddisflies, damselfly nymphs, gnats and chironomids, better known as buzzers. Then, too, there are the patterns that may mimic a wide range of different species but at a shared point in their development. The most common of these are the various emerger patterns, which hang from the water's surface like an insect about to take flight for the first time.

The third group of imitators are those patterns which don't really look like anything in particular, but which have a lifelike (or food-like) quality about them, something in their construction that makes them seem appealing or edible, in ways that can be difficult to elucidate. The spiders would fit within this category – their soft hackles pulse enticingly as they move through the water – and so too would some nymph patterns. They don't so much resemble anything alive as have a life all of their own. I think most of the traditional wet fly patterns could also be categorized in this way, since even those that were designed to look like something in particular (the Black Pennell, for instance, is allegedly a midge imitation, despite being many times too large) don't do a very good job of it. But that doesn't stop them catching fish.

These three quite different approaches to imitation are not just practical divergences. They represent philosophical disagreements. The choices one makes in fly design and selection are a response to questions that one is never fully able to answer. How do fish see colour? How do they select their prey? How fussy are they? What factors might make them reject a fly? What factors make a fly more attractive? And beneath all of this, a bigger one: What is it like to be a trout? Anglers cannot know the answers to these questions, but they must ask them nonetheless, and they must *keep* asking them.

This sense of doubt and ongoing enquiry about why fish bite a hook (and why, just as often, they do not) has – like the false confidence of some – been around for a very long time. In fact, remarkably, the earliest confirmed account of fishing with a fly, written more than eighteen hundred years ago, expresses exactly this uncertainty. In AD 200, the Roman author Claudius Aelianus (or Ælian) described the techniques of Macedonian fishermen, on a river he called Astræus, 'between Berœa and Thessalonica'. There, he said, 'there are fish with speckled skins', which 'feed on a fly peculiar to the country, which hovers on the river'. Those fish were trout, certainly, but what of the insects? It does not look like a wasp, wrote Ælian, 'nor in shape would one justly describe it as a midge or a bee, yet it has something of each of these. In boldness it is like a fly, in size you might call it a midge, it imitates the colour of a wasp, and it hums like a bee.'

These little flies, whatever they might have been, were too delicate to impale on hooks as bait, Ælian explained, but the fishermen had found a solution. 'They fasten red (crimson red) wool round a hook, and fix on to the wool two feathers which grow under a cock's wattles, and which in colour are like wax ... Then they throw their snare, and the fish, attracted and maddened by the colour, comes straight at it, thinking from the pretty sight to get a dainty mouthful; when, however, it opens its jaws, it is caught by the hook and enjoys a bitter repast, a captive.'

So, the ancient Macedonians, in order to tempt trout feeding on tiny yellow and black flies, tied red wool and a couple of grey-brown feathers to a hook. Ælian hedges his bets as to whether hunger or anger caused those trout to bite, but perhaps it hardly matters, because the fishermen caught fish.

When we first moved to Shetland, the most accessible quarry as far as I was concerned – incompetent and largely town-bound as I was – were sillocks, the tiny coalfish or saithe that shoal around the piers in Lerwick Harbour. But while I could see them easily, I still needed a bit of assistance in order to catch them. One of my classmates was a regular at the pier, and he seemed endowed, then, with an almost sacred knowledge of angling. I begged him to share some of that wisdom. 'How can I catch them?' I asked. 'Should I use bait, or spinners, or colourful flies?' His answer surprised me. 'A bare hook is best,' he said. 'Just dangle it in the water and they'll bite.'

Even after thirty years, I can still remember my resistance to that answer, my sense that it couldn't possibly be correct. Even when I tried it for myself, when I saw how the sillocks swarmed around, attracted by the merest glint of metal, I didn't want it to be true. Fishing should be more difficult than that, I thought. It should take more work, more ingenuity. Fish should need fooling, they shouldn't just throw themselves at the hook.

There is, in fly fishing, I think, a similar resistance to simplicity, a commitment to the idea that fish are canny and fastidious, that their capture takes guile and innovation. Some anglers claim that trout will become accustomed to particular fly patterns they see too often, that they will learn to ignore these patterns, understanding the danger they represent. New flies, then, are always needed in order to keep catching. Some anglers claim, either explicitly or by implication, that trout can recognize the subtlest differences in shape and in shade, and that these differences may determine whether a fly will be taken or not. Some anglers claim that when trout are feeding 'selectively' on one particular insect, only a highly accurate imitation of that insect will succeed.

I'm far from convinced that any of this stuff is true.

So far as biologists can tell, a trout's intelligence – in the sense that we humans understand and evaluate it – is roughly equal to that of a frog or a lizard. Delightful, beautiful creatures though they are, and perfectly adapted to the lives they lead, in terms of their mental acuity and their capacity for learning, fish are not evenly matched with human beings. And yet, as any angler knows, half the time they still manage to outwit us. Or they seem to. We cast to them, and they don't bite. All day, sometimes, they ignore our offerings. The rationale for exaggerating their intelligence, then, is obvious. By flattering the fish, anglers are in fact flattering themselves.

In generous terms, the theory of intelligent trout is a way of explaining the unpredictability of angling. In less generous terms, it is just an excuse for our failures. But the excuse doesn't actually add up. Think about it: if a trout is so bright it knows what colour the legs of a *Baetis muticus* mayfly ought to be, and how many segments its abdomen ought to have, then why would it ever take a fly with a long piece of nylon tied to the front and a sharpened hook hanging from its back end? Is the theory that fish are *selectively* selective? Do they fail to notice the hook or the line because they're too busy counting tail filaments and comparing shades of olive? I really don't think so.

Fishing is an activity shot through with doubt. That's one of the things I love most about it: the fact that we never really *know* anything, we can never predict what will happen. The technique and the fly that one day catches fish after fish, the next day might draw a blank. It can be frustrating, yes, but it is also exciting. It keeps us anglers on our toes.

Trout are not really discerning creatures in the way that much angling literature implies. The 'choices' they make – to use a word that may not be wholly appropriate – are part of an ongoing balancing act between two competing instincts: hunger and caution. These impulses, together, are what keep them alive, and the dominance of one or the other will depend on a variety of factors.

To give a simple example: trout in an overcrowded lake will have a suppressed sense of caution in order to have a better chance of satisfying their hunger. They will strike at anything that looks like it might be food because they cannot forgo any opportunities to eat. On the other hand, when there is less competition trout can afford to be more careful, and may reject anything that is not, for certain, edible. They may be spooked by the sight of our line on the water, or an odd, unnatural movement of the fly. They may see the metal of the hook and sense, somehow, that things aren't right. An artificial fly, no matter how well tied, will always be at risk of refusal. In fact, it's remarkable they are not refused more often.

There are times, also, when contradictory factors may be at play. When large numbers of one or two species of insect are coming to the surface at once, for instance, in order to take flight. On these occasions, known as 'hatches', trout may display that well-fed wariness when faced with our patterns, or else they may lose their sense of caution altogether, gorging themselves frantically while the going is good. I have seen both things happen, and it's not always obvious what makes the difference. It is true that at times like these, trout may ignore all food other than those hatching insects. To do so is a useful survival mechanism: a temporary narrowing of the attention.

The received wisdom is that one must imitate the insect at these times, but there is no consensus, naturally, as to what exactly that means. Getting the size right may be an important factor – though flies that are too big or too small are certainly not guaranteed to fail. The shape or posture too is probably of consequence – though fish may be feeding on nymphs, emergers and adults of a species all at once. Colour, some say, really matters – though others say it matters not at all. One other thing is also worth considering: When natural food is abundant, it is easy for your own fly to be lost amid the multitude. So while looking right can help convince the fish to bite, looking wrong can get your fly noticed.

This, I realize, is the opposite of what new anglers want to hear. It is too equivocal, too irresolute. But it's the truth. The fact is that flies can only really be judged on their success on a single occasion, with a single fish: the one that takes. No amount of past successes guarantee that a fly will work today or tomorrow. Likewise, a rejection is not a consequential judgement on a particular pattern (though it may well be a judgement on our technique). Most often we will not know why a fly is turned down, what factor or factors made it fail. When one is throwing hooks at wary fish, rejection inevitably happens.

This is not to say that you cannot improve at choosing flies, at knowing what might work best in any given situation and what can help to trigger a take. You can, of course, and you do. Anglers are always learning. This is to say that there are limits in that direction, that surprise is unavoidable, and that anyone who speaks with absolute certainty about flies is overstepping the line. This is also to say that the choices you make about which patterns to tie and to try are not just a practical matter. They are about the kind of angler you wish to be, and about how you choose to imagine the mind of the fish you seek. This is to say that a creature with a tiny brain, a creature that is probably incapable of genuine discernment, can, in its own native habitat, confound a human being and thwart our intentions. With all our ingenuity and our acumen, it can leave us looking stupid. And isn't that a wonderful, humbling thing? Isn't that what makes this whole enterprise so enthralling, so delightful, so addictive?

Once the first corner of my fly box had been filled with old favourites, I sat down and considered what I ought to tie next. I thumbed through books and browsed websites. I made lists of patterns and materials. I crossed out names and wrote new ones. I changed my mind. And again. What I wanted was a selection that felt deliberate rather than cobbled together, a selection that would cover any angling eventuality I was likely to encounter, but which could be limited to a single box. Or maybe two. (Definitely two.) What I wanted most of all was a selection in which each pattern felt purposeful, and in which each could be tied to my line with confidence. I wanted nothing that would languish unused. I wanted flies that I *liked*.

I knew already what did not appeal to me: the pedantic naturalism that insists on different patterns for every insect species I might meet on river or on loch. I have neither the space nor the entomological knowledge required for this approach, and to be honest I find some of these precise replicas to be sterile, like a photorealist painting of fruit. What interests me most in fly tying, I think, is not the imitation of species but the imitation of life. How does one create something that seems like a bug, even when it looks like nothing in particular? How does one wrap fur and feathers around a hook and make it seem animate?

The spiders fit the bill, and I tied dozens of them – some traditional patterns and a few I invented myself, combining different coloured threads and dubbing with hackles of hen, partridge or starling. I love the uncomplicated beauty of these flies, as I love the very simplest sedge and emerger patterns: just deer's hair and hare's fur, nothing more. As I continued tying, I considered the places I would be fishing, and the flies I would need when I was there. I tried to maintain that functional link between what I was doing at the vice and what I would do at the water. But it wasn't easy.

As an angler, I dream of minimizing even further, of reducing the number of patterns I carry to just a handful of essentials (let's say twelve, shall we, to follow the historical example of *A Treatyse of Fysshynge wyth an Angle*). That way, I could slip a tiny fly box in my pocket and be ready to go. But as a tier, my instincts carried me in the opposite direction. Time and again, I would follow a pattern, make two, three, four flies, and then I would deviate. I would alter the colour of one element or another; I would add something new. Soon enough, I had multiple variants of the same fly, without any particular reason for the difference. I was actively thwarting my own desire for simplicity.

Having snooped into other anglers' fly collections many times over the years, I know that I am not alone in this. The impulse towards proliferation and variation is a strong one, triggered partly by boredom – tying the same fly over and over gets old pretty quick – but by other fac-tors too. Most of all, I think, this impulse is a pre-emptive response to the frustration that every angler knows will come: that moment when everything you throw at the fish is just ignored. That is the time when the scrabble for something else begins, when you search your box for the perfect fly to break the deadlock. Perhaps a flash of orange will make all the difference? Perhaps a longer tail will convince them to bite? And no matter how strongly one believes this stuff to be misguided – and I feel pretty strongly that it is – resistance is close to impossible, both in the moment itself, at the water, and in the anticipation of that moment, at the vice. Because ultimately, fly tying is not just a utilitarian activity but an imaginative one. It is not just about following instructions or providing solutions to problems or even making flies that fish might want to eat. It is about creating something much more important than that.

Ted Leeson wrote that 'A trout fly is only a story we invent, a tale spun on a hook shank from the imperfect materials at hand'. One of the ingredients of those stories – a material that multiplies in the process of tying – is hope. What we make when we sit down with our thread and feathers are beautiful, practical objects. But they are also, each, tiny vessels. Every pattern copied or created, every fly that leaves the vice and is pinned into the box, carries hope inside of it, a hope to which the angler can turn whenever it is needed. It is no won-der, then, that with a packet of hooks in front of us and a box of fur and tinsel, it can be hard to stop tying.

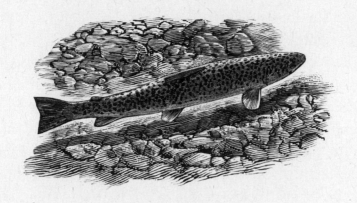

THE
GREEN CREEK

North Island, New Zealand, 2005

NEW ZEALAND IS A LONG way to go to learn a lesson. Especially if, as for me, the journey required to get there – twenty-four hours hurtling through the sky – is spent in a state of ivory-knuckled terror. As I've grown older, my fear of flying, which was once just a minor anxiety, has escalated towards dread. Even the thought of a long-haul flight now, the anticipation of it, will guarantee me a week without sleep. Submitting myself to a whole day in the air, therefore, is a deeply unappealing prospect. But that is what I did. I went, when I was twenty-four, and I learned something about catching fish. And though I loved the place, truly, though it's almost everything I could ask for in a country, there's a good chance that I'll never go back. That journey is just too frightening to consider.

Back then, on that first and only visit, I was there for seven weeks, travelling with Rory and one of our friends, Graeme. We hired a car in Auckland, then drove from campsite to campsite, from the north of the North Island to the south of the South. We shared a cramped three-man tent at night, which felt even smaller during Graeme's regular bouts of parasomnia, when he would shout and swear at the top of his voice without ever waking up. Rory and I found these outbursts exhausting, sometimes shocking, but I suspect those in neighbouring tents may have been even more disturbed than we were.

Our intention on that trip had been to see as much of the country as we could. We had no more plans than that. Back then, in my early twenties, I was fishing far less than I had done in my teens. During four years at university, then another year of teaching overseas, my opportunities were diminished, and my enthusiasm followed. Trout were confined to a few weeks back home each summer.

So when I stepped on the plane to take me to Auckland, fishing just wasn't on my mind. It was January then, the dismal heart of winter.

When I arrived, however, it wasn't winter any more.

Driving around New Zealand as an angler, it's impossible not to think of trout. Every turn in the road reveals a turquoise ribbon of water. Every valley is folded around perfect trout habitat, brimful of life. They are not native here, of course – neither rainbows nor browns – but they have taken to it so wholeheartedly, so successfully, that, like rabbits in the British countryside or starlings in the United States, it is hard now to imagine the place without them.

Rory and I managed five days without fishing rods. Five days of peering over bridges and gazing longingly from car windows. Five days of regretting our short-sightedness in not bringing with us what was so clearly essential. On the sixth day, we walked into a shop in Rotorua and bought everything we needed: the cheapest fly rods, reels and line that we could find, and a handful of flies recommended by the owner.

Looking back, I suspect Graeme's time in New Zealand may have been negatively affected by our inability to resist this particular temptation. Quite a number of our navigational decisions from then on were made on the basis of facts that – for a non-angler such as him – might not have felt pertinent. The proximity of campsites to rivers, for instance. On the other hand, sitting bolt upright and yelling obscenities in the middle of the night can have a negative effect on those who share a tent with you. So perhaps, after all, we were even.

Fishing for trout in New Zealand, it turned out, demanded quite different skills from those at which we had any degree of proficiency. Precise casting with dry flies in fast-flowing water was not something either of us had had much practice at, and it showed. We fished fairly often, but we caught next to nothing. We saw trout, naturally – saw them rising and swirling, and finning in clear pools – but we struggled to see them any closer than that. Every now and then, one of the less discerning individuals would rise to a fly we had cast, and we would snatch it impatiently, prematurely from their mouths. The line would land back in a heap at our feet before the fish even had a chance to close its jaws.

On one of our earliest outings, at a creek in the North Island, we got our first good look at one of these big New Zealand trout. We had realized by then that fish in that country did not conform to the same rules of growth as those we knew from home. New Zealand trout, it seems, are born large, then get larger very quickly. Almost all the ones we saw, and certainly the very few we caught, were more substantial than any we had seen in Shetland before.

The creek – the name of which is long lost to my memory – was very green. It had steep, grassy banks on one side and overhanging trees on the other, and the water itself was a rich, cabbagey hue. It was clear enough to see the bottom, except in the deepest pools; yet it was plainly, unmistakably green.

The creek was also narrow, and slow-moving too, which allowed us to cast from one side to the other, and to convince ourselves that we were doing it well. The fact that it was the middle of the day, with bright, baking sunshine, and we could see no fish feeding, did not deter us at all. We just cast and kept casting.

We found one fish in the end: a brown trout, holding still in deep water, on the inner edge of an elbow in the stream. It was lying close against a high bank, and from the rocks above we peered down at it, like children throwing sticks over a bridge. We couldn't cast to it, though. There was nowhere to stand nearby from where our lines could reach it. So for a time we just watched, saw the slow curve and flicker of its body, as it held itself steady in the current.

We wondered after a while if there might be something wrong. Trout are wary creatures, and we hadn't exactly been subtle in our staring. Surely it had noticed us gazing down from above? But it stayed where it was, barely moving. Was it ill, perhaps? Or was it just resting, waiting for the heat of the day to pass?

It was inevitable we would try our luck, and I don't apologize for that. Anyone else would have done the same. For though we couldn't quite *cast* to the fish, that didn't mean we couldn't get our hooks in front of it. We took turns, lowering our lines straight down, as we used to do from the pier as children. We tried floating flies first, letting them drift above the trout, then flicking them upstream again each time those flies were ignored. We changed patterns. Then again. Then we switched to sinking flies. This time it seemed we might have more luck. While trying to convince a fish to come to the surface when it's not actively feeding may not succeed, putting food in front of its face, taking all of the effort away, could easily have a different outcome.

Or maybe not.

Time after time, our flies drifted so close to the trout's nose that all it had to do was yawn and we'd be connected. But the fish stayed put and its mouth stayed shut. Once or twice, the hooks bumped against its skin, and we saw it flinch, then settle back into position, but it showed no more interest than that. We had run out of flies and run out of ideas.

If I said that I didn't expect what happened next, it wouldn't be entirely truthful. We were frustrated, and had exhausted all legitimate options. The fish seemed almost to be taunting us, staying in full view, but refusing to cooperate. And yet we kept going, kept dropping our flies in front it.

What happened next was almost inevitable.

The reason it makes sense to talk of angling as a *sport* is not because fisher and fish are opponents in some kind of match. To frame it in such a way is to seriously misinterpret what's going on. A fish cannot give consent to 'play', for one thing, and the stakes are far too high on their end for it to ever be anything like a game. No, the sport of angling comes from the fact it has rules: rules that make its objectives more difficult to achieve than they otherwise would be.

Golf would be a great deal easier if you could just pick up the ball, walk to the green, and drop it down the hole. Tennis would be a much less challenging activity if you didn't have to deal with somebody else on the other side of the net, hitting things back at you. Likewise, fishing doesn't need to be as difficult as we make it. Dynamite, tossed into the water, is a much more effective way to catch fish than a rod and line. So too are gillnets and electric probes.

To be an angler is to accept the voluntary binding of

one's own hands. It is to accept a set of limitations, a series of essentially arbitrary customs that dictate what can and cannot be done in order to catch fish 'sportingly'.

One of those customs is that fish should be hooked only by the mouth.

Some people take this rule very seriously indeed. A fish that is 'foul hooked', some say – that is, caught on a part of the body other than the lips or mouth – must be returned to the water. It should not be counted in competitions. It should not be counted as part of a daily tally (if one keeps such a thing). It should not be considered *caught* at all, in fact. It might as well never have happened.

I'm not nearly so strict as this. The majority of fish that are hooked this way – usually in the base of a fin or the tail, though it can be just about anywhere – are caught because they tried to take a fly but missed the target. Perhaps they turned at the last moment, or else thrashed at what they thought was food in order to stop it from moving. Either way, they were fooled, and to get too pedantic about such things seems needless to me. I would much rather catch a fish the correct way, certainly, but I'm not going to beat myself up about the occasional one that comes in backwards.

This particular situation was different, though, since the trout had not at any stage mistaken our flies for food. Indeed, it had demonstrated excellent judgement throughout this encounter. Its only error had been to lie in full view of a pair of over-eager young anglers above. But that was error enough.

After yet one more refusal, I lifted my rod and the hook found something solid. The fish moved fast, and the line in my hands went with it. The rod tip bent over as the full weight of the trout became apparent.

I knew it was foul-hooked immediately, but for the next few minutes I wasn't thinking about that detail. I was just trying not to lose it, trying to guide it safely to shore. The detail returned, however, when the fish was in my hands. A long, pale trout, bright gold across the back, with a mouth altogether too large for its body. It wasn't the prettiest I'd ever caught, but it was, at that time, the biggest. And it was hooked in the corner of a pectoral fin.

The elation that would otherwise have accompanied a catch like that was instead muted, almost absent, and as I stooped to release it back into the creek I felt a twinge of something uncomfortable. It was the same kind of twinge, I suppose, that I might feel after winning a quiz by searching for the answers online. Was it guilt? Or shame? Not quite, but close. It was a feeling of deflation and of undeserved success.

What I learned from this experience, I really ought to have known already. But it's a lesson that young people can be reluctant to believe. It is that rules – even arbitrary ones – do not always stand in the way of pleasure. Sometimes, it turns out, they define it. Sometimes the rules really matter.

It was nearly three weeks before either of us caught another fish.

KEEP
OUT!

YOU CAN TELL A GREAT deal about the social history of angling by walking into a tackle shop in Britain or North America. Look at how things are arranged around the store. Notice who is present and who is not. Exclusion and division have long been part of this sport. Some people have been discouraged or prevented from taking part; some have been relegated to fishing certain waters and for certain species deemed to be of lower status. And while much of the elitism and discrimination that were once widespread have now faded, their repercussions have not.

It didn't have to be this way. Fishing ought to be a supremely egalitarian hobby, since it can provide food as well as pleasure. It is not necessarily a *cheap* hobby, but it needn't be overly expensive either. The basic equipment required can quite easily be cobbled together, as any child with a bamboo cane for a rod and a bent pin for a hook is well aware. But it's a hobby upon which social pressures have been applied, in ways that have distorted both how it is practised and how it is understood. One of those pressures, unsurprisingly, has been around class.

From the very earliest literature on the subject, a distinction was made between fishing as recreation and as subsistence. In 1496, *A Treatyse of Fysshynge wyth an Angle* declared that 'you must not use this aforesaid artful sport for covetousness to increasing or saving of your money'. Instead, angling was to be pursued 'principally for your solace, and to bring health to your body, and especially to your soul'.

It's impossible to know the extent to which this distinction would have made sense to those who fished at the time the *Treatyse* was published. Virtually the only evidence of angling that remains from those times is in writing, and since literacy was limited almost exclusively to the rich, writing cannot tell the whole story. It is certain, however, that poorer people would have supplemented their diets with fish, wherever they had access to water. Some would have used nets, some would have used traps or spears, and some, no doubt, would have used hooks. It is quite likely, in fact, that until the late Middle Ages fishing with rod and line was most commonly done by the lower classes. And while hunger would have driven much of this activity, that does not mean those who fished did not also enjoy it. Surely, they often did.

But in Britain and mainland Europe, this food-gathering technique was, around this time, beginning to be rarefied in print. If it was not already a popular leisure pursuit for the wealthy, it was certainly becoming one. Indeed, the authors of some of the earliest European angling books were engaged in something like an advertising campaign, extolling the noble virtues of the sport – comparing it favourably to hunting and falconry. One of the key aims of these books, according to the environmental historian Richard C. Hoffmann, was 'to promote the participation of the social elite'.

At the same time, there is also evidence of efforts to *limit* participation at the other end of the economic spectrum, to keep knowledge of angling methods away from the masses. When the *Treatyse of Fysshynge wyth an Angle* was first printed, for instance, it was bound together with a significantly larger work, the *Boke of St Albans*. There was thematic logic in this decision, since the subject matter of that book – hunting, hawking and heraldry – aligned quite neatly with that of the *Treatyse*. But the real reason, according to the man who printed the book, Wynkyn de Worde, was to make the whole package more expensive, so that 'idle persons, who would have little moderation in the sport of fishing, shall not utterly destroy it'.

Already, then, a process of stratification was underway, a division between those who fished and who needed to eat their catch, and those who fished but could afford not to. Those in the latter camp were constructing an elaborate sporting culture out of what, for others, was an aid to survival. In doing so, they wove the social divisions and prejudices of the time into the very fabric of angling. Those divisions, among and between anglers, would evolve over the coming centuries – but they would persist.

At the bottom of our garden, here in central Scotland, is a river. At night, in bed, I can hear the messy whisper of the water, like a hundred conversations happening at once. Even now, sitting at my desk with the windows closed against the early-spring chill, that sound is present; and if I stop typing for a moment it rises to fill the space. Most days, my partner and I take a walk along the banks, half a mile upstream, across a narrow bridge, then half a mile back. We pause to look at birds, or else just pause to make the walk last longer.

I don't know what the fishing is like in this river, or whether it has a healthy population of trout. Despite its proximity, I have never once cast a line here, and it's possible that I never will. For now, I do all my fishing elsewhere.

The cost of river fishing in this part of Scotland varies enormously, and so far as I can tell, the key determinant for this variation is the presence or absence of Atlantic salmon. I can get a full season's permit on a river about ten miles away for the price of a heavy hardback book. It is an excellent place to catch brown trout, but the run of salmon is small, unpredictable, and limited to the end of the season. The river at the bottom of our garden, on the other hand, though not one of this country's many legendary rivers, still has a reliable run of salmon, and costs eight times as much. While trout are caught, they are, so far as I can tell, a species of secondary interest to many anglers here.

It's not that the price of fishing in this river is out of my reach, as it would be in those more famous places. What I object to, rather, is the enormous discrepancy, and the fact that it rests upon the social prestige that one species has been granted over another. That prestige and its complicated historical legacies are made explicit by the fact that the right to fish for salmon in about sixty rivers across Scotland – including this one – still belongs exclusively to 'the Crown' (in other words, the reigning monarch). Those rights are then leased to angling associations, who pass on the costs to their members.

The irony is that these royal rivers actually offer some of the most affordable salmon fishing in the country, since the Crown Estate leases its rights to local clubs, rather than to the highest bidder. In rivers where those rights belong to landowners, or where they are sold separately from the land, it is often only the very wealthy who can afford to fish. And this has long been the case. Salmon, this enigmatic species – which is essentially just a brown trout's big, restless cousin – has, in angling lore, been elevated above all others. The 'king of fish', some call it, emphasizing even further that peculiar, regal status. The fact that Atlantic salmon have been disappearing for well over a century, and that their numbers are now perilously low in many rivers, has done nothing to diminish the demand from some anglers for exclusivity. Quite the opposite.

Really, I should just get over myself and buy a membership for the river at the bottom of the garden, or even just a day ticket or two. It wouldn't exactly break the bank. My refusal to do so – on principle, I tell myself – achieves absolutely nothing. And to be honest, sometimes what I refer to as 'principle' is really just curmudgeonliness, compounded by a limited income. I'm missing out for no good reason.

As the sport of angling grew in popularity from the Middle Ages onwards, the right to cast one's line in a particular piece of water became a commodity. That right could be owned exclusively, and could be used in turn to exclude. During the eighteenth century, in Britain, this exclusion – the squeezing out of poorer anglers – became systematic. The various processes of 'enclosure', by which land (and water) that once had been unfenced and used in common was handed over to rich private landlords, transformed the lives of a significant part of the population. Many people lost their homes, their livelihoods, their sources of food. Some emigrated, some moved into towns and cities, providing a workforce for the new factories of the Industrial Revolution. The loss of a right to fish, then, was just one in a great litany of losses, but it was no less consequential for that. The passing of the infamous Black Act, in 1723, meant that the punishment for those who fished in someone else's pond or river without permission could be death.

The various efforts to prevent or discourage poor people from angling never entirely succeeded, of course. Some found ways, illicit or otherwise. But the vast economic inequalities that limited people's access to water ensured that the sport was dominated by the upper and middle classes, right up until the nineteenth century. Then, in Britain, something peculiar happened. A split emerged in the sport, a wholly eccentric division between two kinds of fish and two kinds of fishing: 'coarse' and 'game'. It is a split that makes no real sense, except when viewed through the prism of class.

The difference between coarse fish and game fish is mostly just a matter of palatability. Though many coarse species, such as carp, bream and pike, were once widely eaten, by the 1800s they were generally considered less tasty – *coarse*, in other words – and more difficult to prepare than game fish: trout, salmon, char and grayling. There are other differences, too, though none are especially important. In terms of anatomy, game fish possess an extra fin, the adipose, a little nub located between the tail and the dorsal fin; and coarse fish tend to have larger scales. In habitat, trout prefer cold, highly oxygenated water, whereas coarse fish, for the most part, will happily live in sun-baked ponds, sluggish rivers and canals. And as far as technique is concerned, the use of artificial flies was becoming the tactic of choice for many who pursued trout and salmon in the nineteenth century, whereas bait was most often used for other species.

These distinctions had never previously meant much at all, and they have no inherent significance for the angler. But from the mid-nineteenth century, in Britain, the sport of freshwater fishing was firmly bisected, and the catalyst for this rupture was social change. Increasingly, working-class men were allowed regular leisure time – a partial weekend – and were encouraged by trade unions, temperance societies and civic leaders to spend their Saturday afternoons on wholesome activities: gardening, team sports, museum visits, countryside pursuits. There was undoubtedly an element of social control behind this urging; the organizations and authorities promoting these activities were eager for working men to become, variously, more respectable, more sober, and less likely to revolt. But regardless of the intention, these 'rational recreations', as they were sometimes known, were taken up with enormous enthusiasm. And fishing, along with football, was among the most popular of all. By pooling their financial resources with angling association membership fees, it became possible for poorer anglers to lease fishing rights in waterways that were accessible by foot or by train from industrial towns and cities. Some of these associations boasted thousands of members, sometimes tens of thousands, who would compete against each other in weekly fishing matches, in which catches were returned alive to the water. This was the birth of contemporary coarse angling.

Although the social divisions between the two forms of freshwater fishing were never absolute – there were always some middle- and upper-class anglers who continued to pursue coarse species, and in parts of the UK the opportunity to fish for trout would have been available to poorer people – a stratification had unquestionably emerged. Coarse fishing became overwhelmingly a working-class hobby, limited to lakes, canals and rivers that could be accessed by public transport, while game fishing took place principally in rural areas, and was financially out of reach for most people. The social structure of a nation came to be reflected in its own water, with coarse fish at the bottom, trout in the middle, and salmon at the top.

This split has never gone away. Coarse and game angling, in Britain, are still largely separate pursuits. But their relationship to class has eroded. Salmon have retained their status above all other species – a status evidenced by the costs associated with fishing for them – but coarse fishing has shaken off any stigma it may once have held, and affordable trout angling has become widely available.

To a remarkable degree, in fact, fishing has moved on from its unequal past, and is now genuinely class-diverse. A survey of around 2,400 UK anglers, in 2009, showed that participants in both branches of the sport came from right across the social spectrum. And while those with the very highest incomes were more likely to be game anglers, and those with the very lowest were more likely to be coarse anglers, the differences were otherwise minimal. In the US, meanwhile, there is no directly comparable division to that between game and coarse angling in the UK (though the distinction between fly and bait fishing is not dissimilar). There, too, people of all incomes participate to a similar degree in angling.

Scanning the various surveys of those who fish, from both sides of the Atlantic, one thing is immediately apparent. While the class background of anglers seems, these days, to be exceptionally diverse, gender is another matter entirely. Statistics on the participation of women in the UK vary somewhat, most likely because the numbers involved are so low. However, both the 2009 survey, mentioned above, and the National Angling Survey, published in 2012 (which had more than 27,000 respondents), found that fewer than 3 per cent of anglers were women.

That number, shocking though it ought to be, will not really surprise anyone who fishes regularly. You don't need statistics to know just how rare female anglers are. To put that rarity in a personal context, I can say that, to the best of my recollection, in the past thirty years I have never seen a woman fishing without a male partner. Not once. And I can probably count on my fingers the number of women I've seen fishing at all. Anglers can become inured to this massive gender imbalance, but I think it's important to be reminded of just how weird it is, of just how strange for a hobby – from which women are neither banned nor, any longer, systematically discouraged from taking part – to be so overwhelmingly dominated by men.

Interestingly, in the United States things are much less uneven. According to a 2016 US government report, based on a survey of 30,000 people, a quarter of all anglers there are women; a more recent survey, by the Outdoor Foundation, found it was more than a third. This enormous discrepancy between participation in the US and the UK suggests that the traditional explanation for the lack of female anglers – that women are somehow 'naturally' disinclined to fish – is shaky at best. Clearly, there are other factors at work.

So what then are those factors? Why are women such a minority among anglers? How has this imbalance been created and how is it perpetuated?

The answers are not hard to find.

Though women are and have long been massively under-represented within angling, they are not completely absent from the history of the sport. Until quite recently, for instance, *A Treatyse of Fysshynge wyth an Angle* was credited to a nun by the name of Dame Juliana Berners. And though scholars now consider that attribution to be an error, the prioress is still, and probably always will be, the person most closely associated with that text.

There are two particular fields, though, within which women have had striking historical successes. The first of these, in Britain, is Atlantic salmon fishing. A century ago, three female anglers broke national records that still stand today. In October of 1922, Georgina Ballantine, in the River Tay, caught the biggest salmon ever to be landed in the UK with rod and line. It weighed 64lbs. The following year, Doreen Davey caught Britain's biggest ever spring-run salmon, in the River Wye, at 59lbs. And the year after that, Clementina Morison caught the largest salmon ever to be landed on a fly, in the Deveron, in north-east Scotland. That fish weighed 61lbs. These extraordinary catches, which will likely never be bettered, led some male anglers to grumble that women might have an unfair advantage when it came to salmon. Pheromones, they claimed, rubbed off on to the bait or fly, might be behind these successes. It's an argument that sounds a bit like science, but is really just condescension.

The other field in which women have traditionally excelled is fly tying. On both sides of the Atlantic, some of the most famous tiers historically have been female. Among them is Mary Orvis Marbury, whose *Favorite Flies and Their Histories* (1892) helped to standardize American fly patterns, and remains one of the most important, most popular, and most beautifully illustrated books ever published on the subject. Then there was Elizabeth Greig, described by the *New Yorker* magazine in 1942 as 'the fastest trout-fly tier in the nation'; this, despite the fact she held each one between thumb and forefinger as it was constructed, rather than using a vice. In Scotland, Megan Boyd became famous for tying extravagant salmon flies for clients such as Prince Charles, and was widely considered to be among the very best in the world. The author and editor David Profumo called Boyd's flies 'the Fabergés of the fishing world'.

It is not a coincidence that women have been most prominent historically in these two fields – Atlantic salmon fishing and fly tying – for these are the fields in which women have most consistently been allowed, or even encouraged, to take part. Tying flies, as a skilled and delicate craft, was never thought of as inappropriate work for women, and companies producing flies for sale often had exclusively female staff. Many of these tiers – and Megan Boyd was one – would never have actually cast their own creations.

Salmon fishing in Britain has traditionally been subject to quite different social pressures from other forms of angling, since its participants came largely from the aristocracy and the upper middle classes. Whereas working-class women were very often unable to participate in hobbies outside the home, with time as limited a resource as money, the women of wealthy families often had leisure time galore. Just as rich men could abandon children and other domestic inconveniences for the pleasures of the riverside, so too – with nannies, cooks and maids at their disposal – could some rich women.

But the gentrified world of Victorian salmon angling was also very different in terms of its gender norms and expectations from, for instance, the working-class world of coarse angling in the same era. The latter was focused heavily on competition, on regular fishing matches, and was centred, socially, in pubs and working men's clubs. It was accessible only through membership of fishing associations, which, by custom or regulation, did not admit women. Salmon fishing, on the other hand, was imagined as a sophisticated and genteel pastime, to which the key excluding factor was money rather than gender. And while it was still a sport enjoyed principally by gentlemen, it was possible for women to get involved without being considered too unladylike.

Salmon fishing, then, was an exception. For the most part, in Britain, until the late twentieth century, women rarely fished, were actively discouraged or forbidden from doing so, and their absence from the sport provided the false logic used to justify their continued exclusion. Women didn't fish, therefore fishing was for men, therefore women shouldn't fish. Etcetera.

There are still many who cling to an updated version of this logic, who argue that the lack of female anglers today is evidence only that women are not interested in angling, that they *just don't like this kind of thing*. Often, this argument will be framed in vaguely genetic terms, or will make reference to a 'hunting instinct', a throwback to our prehistoric selves that lurks only within men, leading them to chase and kill animals for pleasure. To say that the science behind these claims is fuzzy would be a major understatement, for there is fierce disagreement among biologists, neuroscientists and psychologists about the extent to which behaviours and traits can be ascribed to inherent differences between the sexes.

For me, the idea that gender imbalances in angling can be explained away biologically is far from convincing, not least because of that striking disparity between female participation in Britain and the United States – a disparity that exists within Europe, too. In France, for instance, female anglers make up only 3 per cent of the total, whereas in Sweden, Norway and Finland it is around a third. These enormous differences are proof that cultural factors are at work, and that women's near absence from the sport is not inevitable. I would take my scepticism even further, however, and question the characterization of angling that lies at the heart of the hunting instinct argument. To put it simply: if the need to hunt really were in men's blood and bones, if they were driven to act out ancient brutal urges, it just doesn't seem likely to me that sitting on the banks of a canal with a twelve-metre roach pole, or casting tiny dry flies to brown trout in a stream, would satisfy that need. These are quiet, slow activities, no more akin to chasing and slaughtering a woolly mammoth than pottery or contemporary dance. And even if they did somehow scratch a hunting itch, that wouldn't tell half the story. The pleasures of angling are complicated, they are multifarious, and to try and boil everything down to one inherited impulse is to miss almost all of what's going on.

In the United States, far more than in Britain, fishing does remain part of a broader and more entrenched hunting culture (or at least a culture that *includes* hunting), one that has its roots in that country's own historical self-image. Consciously or not, anglers in the US participate in and perpetuate a story of the American 'outdoorsman' that harks back to colonial legends of the frontier. It is a story that makes sense today only because of the extent of land that remains undeveloped, and the extent of water that remains public and accessible. Given this intimate link between fishing, hunting, national identity and masculinity, then, it might seem odd that women have played a more prominent role in American angling than British – and certainly it offers yet more evidence against the instinct argument. But there are good reasons for the difference. Historically, fishing in the US has been both more democratic, in terms of who could fish where, and also more individualistic – less reliant on club membership, in other words. These two factors combined have made the exclusion of women less consistent than in the UK. If an American woman in the nineteenth or early twentieth century really wanted to fish, and didn't much care what anyone else thought about it, she was often able to do so.

In Britain, on the other hand, angling culture was tied to socioeconomic identities that were shared and delimited, and for the great majority participation required membership of associations, the rules of which reflected the social prejudices of the time. If a British woman really wanted to fish, she either needed to be rich or to beg for permission from men. The nature of land and water ownership in Britain, in other words, and the deeply classed history of the sport in this country, is probably responsible for the much lower participation of women in angling in the UK than in the United States.

Within all three of the angling traditions mentioned here – upper-class British, working-class British and American – fishing was considered to be an activity to which women were not naturally inclined. Each of these traditions projected its own ideas of masculinity on to the sport, its own notions of what kind of man a fisher ought to be. There was the refined gentleman salmon angler, the fiercely competitive and sociable coarse angler, and the lone, rugged outdoorsman, wandering the American wilderness. The funny thing was, not only were each of these imagined archetypes quite different, but each, to some extent, contradicted the others. Anglers were convinced that manliness mattered, they just couldn't agree on what it looked like.

Times have changed. Of course they have. Today, with a few anachronistic exceptions on both sides of the Atlantic, women are no longer excluded from angling associations, and those who wish to fish can do so with as much ease, in theory, as men. What's more, even among those who believe that women are innately uninterested in fishing, you'd be hard pressed to find anyone who thought they should be *prevented* from doing so. In fact, many fishing clubs and organizations have actively tried to recruit women and girls as members. They have promoted angling as an inclusive activity, a hobby suitable for anyone with an interest in water and what it holds. Yet, as the statistics demonstrate, those efforts – in Britain and parts of Europe, at least – have had very limited success. So what is going on?

The explanation, I think, is simple. It is that social exclusions perpetuate themselves, and they do so even when the most rigid barriers to participation are removed. There are few female anglers now because women were discouraged or prevented from taking part in the past. Merely changing the rules and lifting the prohibitions doesn't lead to equal access. Few women fish, therefore few women take up fishing.

There are reasons this process of ongoing exclusion is worse in angling than in many other activities. There is, for example, the fact that angling – unlike, say, hiking or swimming – is a fairly complicated hobby to take up. The start-up costs are not inconsiderable, and some initial instruction is very often required. Most anglers begin in childhood, and they do so by borrowing someone else's equipment, by sitting with them and learning from them. That someone, very often, is a parent. If fathers choose to take their sons but not their daughters fishing, then those girls are unlikely to ever take it up themselves. Similarly, if anglers choose not to invite their female partners or friends fishing, those women may never have the chance to try it.

Then, too, there is the amount of time that angling can take up, versus the uneven distribution of household labour. Despite positive changes in recent decades, women continue to be responsible for more housework and childcare overall than men. This leaves them, inevitably, with less time to spare. As the author, editor and angler Kate Fox has written, 'Provide child care and housecleaning services to women interested in fly fishing, and the ranks will swell accordingly.'

But perhaps the simplest and most significant factor discouraging women from fishing is that, looking in from the outside, it still appears to be very much a man's realm. Indeed, it still *is* very much a man's realm. As with other outdoor pursuits, fishing alone may not feel safe for many women, and certainly may not feel comfortable. Likewise, the benefits of belonging to a community of anglers – within a fishing club, for instance – may not appeal to women if that community is exclusively, or almost exclusively, male. The current demographics of the sport will in this way shape the future demographics. Adults take up this or that hobby in part because they can imagine themselves as the kind of person who does this or that activity. Identity is always part of the equation. If women never see other women fishing, if every book on the subject is written by and about men, if tackle companies promote their products with only men in mind, it is exceedingly hard for women to see themselves as potential anglers.

For young children, identity, in this sense, matters less. My eldest niece asked for a fishing rod for her sixth birthday – a pink one – because she wanted to join her dad, my brother, on some of his angling excursions. It delights me that this choice was so simple for her, so obvious, and that it hasn't yet occurred to her that girls and boys might pursue different pastimes. Sadly, even if she persists with fishing, even if she enjoys it as much as her father does, I am certain that, in a few years' time, her peers will let her know exactly what girls should or should not be doing. Nobody enforces gender norms more insistently or cruelly than adolescents.

Most of the disincentives for women and girls who might otherwise take up angling work in similar ways to exclude those from other under-represented groups, especially people from ethnic minority backgrounds.* In Britain and the United States, anglers are much whiter, statistically speaking, than society as a whole. Fewer than 1 per cent of respondents to the National Angling Survey, for instance, identified themselves as coming from an ethnic minority background, compared to around 13 per cent of the UK population overall.

This imbalance has its roots in patterns of immigration, and in the racism that many immigrants, historically, have suffered. In the UK and Europe, black and Asian populations have overwhelmingly settled in urban places. Employment opportunities were one reason for this, but 'safety and community in numbers', as the psychotherapist Beth Collier has put it, were an even more significant factor. Though many immigrants arrived from rural parts of the world – and though many, surely, would once have fished – it was cities that provided partial sanctuary from the hostility they experienced upon arrival. In time, the cultures of these minorities became urbanized, and many came to see the countryside as an unsafe place, where people of colour were more liable to encounter abuse.

The legacies of this are clear. Today, young people

---

* These demographic barriers do not extend, it seems, to those with disabilities. According to the National Angling Survey of 2012, nearly 20 per cent of anglers have an illness or disability that affects their physical activity. Many commercial fishing venues, which might not otherwise be accessible to those with limited mobility, offer wheelchair access to the waterside.

from ethnic minority backgrounds are less likely to be taken fishing because their parents are less likely to fish. And for those who do take an interest in the sport, or in other rural activities, an uncomfortable sense of 'hyper-visibility' can await: a feeling of standing out, of looking different to those around you, and of being noticed because of that difference. This feeling is not just a matter of conspicuousness, needless to say; people of colour are still sometimes treated as though they don't belong in the countryside, or as though they are a threat. And for many, it is preferable to avoid that discomfort, that anxiety, altogether.

There is one place, however, where the world of angling does appear more representative of society, both in terms of gender and of ethnic background, and that's online. Though there are plenty of websites and forums where the worst elements of the sport – sexist, sometimes racist – can still be seen, there are many others that are welcoming and diverse, or that are aimed specifically at minority anglers.

Social media too provides a platform where some of the imbalances of angling culture can, to a degree, be redressed. Women are responsible for some of the most popular Instagram angling accounts, for instance, both in the US and in the UK. While novelty may be part of the appeal in some cases, a great many of these accounts are run by women who have also made names for themselves offline, as broadcasters, writers, guides and instructors. There are, in addition, a multitude of accounts providing online communities for women who fish, and others that are doing the same for anglers from ethnic minorities.

All of these online spaces are changing the image of angling, more quickly than would ever be possible offline. They are reshaping what an 'average angler' is understood to look like, and casting off some of the unwanted cultural and social baggage the sport still carries. They are doing a pretty good job of it, too, and I suspect that in the coming years the effects will increasingly become apparent. Women who want to fish – particularly young women and girls – will have role models and guides to whom they can turn. Likewise, anglers from ethnic minority backgrounds. They will be reassured that this is a hobby suitable for people like them. They will feel less out of place and more welcome by the water.

I hope, sincerely, that by the time my niece – now eagerly casting with her father – feels the social pressure to give up and do something more 'girly', she might find herself not just *able* to resist, but *encouraged*.

THE
RIVER DEVON

Clackmannanshire, 2020

THERE IS NO SUCH THING as a complete angler, and for the most part I'm glad of that. Angling comprises a set of skills which one can improve over time. Competence can develop into expertise, and observation can crystallize into knowledge. But that knowledge and expertise are invariably bounded. An angler's experience will be limited to certain species of fish, certain techniques, certain types of water. Which means there is always the opportunity, even after many decades of fishing, to throw oneself back in at the deep end, and to become again a beginner.

Growing up in Shetland was an immense luxury as far as fishing was concerned. To have access to trout water of such quality, and in such quantity, is rare, and even in my youth I did not take it for granted. But even so, fishing in Shetland is in some ways restricted. For one thing, the only species of any interest to fly fishers is brown trout (including a population of sea trout that is these days pretty unreliable). For another thing, the islands don't have any rivers. Not one. In fact, they don't even have any streams large enough that one might, over-generously, *mistake* for a river. What they have are lochs. Many, many lochs.

When I moved away from Shetland in my thirties, therefore, I found myself at something of a disadvantage. Where I live now, in central Scotland, much of the best trout fishing happens in running water. To stick only with what I knew would be to miss out, and for a few years, that's what I did. I missed out. I tried one or two reservoirs, one or two 'put and take' fisheries, and I didn't think that much of any of them. I fished less often than I ever had before, and I wondered if the enthusiasm might be leaving me for good. Now and then I visited a river – usually at someone else's invitation – and I did my best to translate my skills to this unfamiliar water. But always I had the sense of being a total amateur, the sense that thirty years of angling experience were of no help whatsoever. And my catches on these occasions usually reflected that helplessness. Once or twice I had a spot of unexpected luck. But mostly I just splashed about and then went home, feeling like a fool.

It's not that I didn't know the basics of river fishing. Over the years, I'd accumulated scraps of knowledge on the subject – from books, mostly. It's just that faced with an actual river, a real live piece of water, flowing in front of me, I couldn't summon any confidence. I felt intimidated. I did what I thought was right, from memory and from intuition. Then, far too quickly, I would revert to the comfort of those techniques I knew best. I would fish the river as though it were a loch, and that just doesn't work.

Eventually, I decided that enough was enough. I live in easy reach of some excellent trout fishing, and I wanted to make use of it. I gave myself a pep talk. I am not incompetent, I said (with limited conviction). I am capable of learning.

What I wanted to learn, specifically, were those methods most unfamiliar to me: the various deep-water techniques that, bundled together, are sometimes labelled 'Euro nymphing'. In fact, at this stage, I wasn't too interested in the 'various' side of things. I felt no pressing need to distinguish French from Spanish or Polish from Czech nymphing. What I wanted, for the time being, was just to make a start, to get a sense of how these tactics work. So I read some articles and I tied some flies, and I bought a club membership for the River Devon.

FIRST VISIT

On a map, the Devon is an odd-looking river. From its source in the Ochil Hills, not far from Gleneagles, it flows east, through two, then three reservoirs, before seeming to change its mind about where it wants to go. At the Crook of Devon it abruptly changes course, heading west, just the other side of those same hills in which it first began. Though the river is thirty-three miles in length, its end point, where it meets the River Forth, just west of Alloa, is less than six miles from its source.

The lower half of the Devon, from Castlehill Reservoir onwards, has a healthy population of brown trout, once topped up by stocking, but now self-sustaining. It is also incredibly diverse, from rushing waterfalls and tiny shaded pools, to wide, languorous stretches through the floodplain east of Stirling. Some of the river is easily accessible, popular with walkers as well as anglers. Other parts are overgrown and near-impossible to reach. Despite its proximity to towns and villages along its length, the Devon is home to a host of wildlife, including beavers, which have been quietly but steadily recolonizing the rivers of central Scotland for years now.

My first attempt to fish the Devon was poorly timed. A thunderstorm and heavy fall of rain had brought water levels way up. I kept an eye on the level gauge online, saw it rise rapidly then just as soon begin to fall. I waited twenty-four hours, and figured that might be enough. I was impatient. I was prepared to take a chance.

I drove east, to the village of Dollar, then a little way beyond. Down a narrow, snaking road, I stopped beside a bridge and parked. The river was loud as I set up the rod, tied on my flies, and stepped into my waders. Trees overhung everything, a dense canopy of late summer green that held much of the morning light at bay. I took a path that led upstream and knew immediately that I'd been too optimistic. The water was still very high and was churned into a muddy, murky brown, the colour of tea with just a splash of milk.

It was not inviting, and nor did it look easy to fish. I tried to move a bit farther upstream, but my way was blocked by thick vegetation on land and by the heavy rush of the water. I made a few desultory casts, then figured downstream might be more accommodating, so went back up and over the road. I found a spot below the bridge and stepped in.

There is a feeling that comes when wading in running water. The pressure, at first, is against you. It makes all movement awkward and unsteady. There is the sense of being unwelcome, of being shoved out of the way. The river has somewhere to go, and it will take you with it if it can. But stop, stand, make yourself solid, and things begin to change. Rather than push against you, the current absorbs your form. It flows around you. There is an easing in that moment that feels something like acceptance, as if the river has allowed you to remain.

I let my feet settle in among the unseen stones, then unhooked the tail fly from the rod and made my first real cast, just upstream. I aimed to one side of the central current, in what might have been slack water on another day, but which then was only marginally less torrential than the rest. The flies plopped into the swirling pool and rushed back towards me in seconds. I cast again.

The basic logic of deep-water nymphing is that trout do

most of their feeding on the bottom, therefore the bottom is where our hooks ought to be. Heavy patterns, weighted with lead or tungsten, are required. These sink quickly and maximize the time the flies spend in front of the fish, thereby maximizing the chances of catching them.

There are a few problems with this logic, though. One of which is that traditional fly line gets dragged around by surface currents, making those flies behave unnaturally and unappealingly beneath the water. To avoid this, anglers have to keep that thick fly line off the surface as much as possible, using a long leader – the supple, intermediate section between fly line and tippet – which cuts through the current.

The next problem is knowing when a fish takes. Since you are not actively retrieving, as in wet fly fishing, and cannot see your hook, as in dry fly fishing, the usual indications are not available. Some nymphing techniques involve casting very short distances and maintaining a tight enough line that you can *feel* any bites as the fly bounces along the riverbed. Others require brightly coloured leaders, so you can *see* any twitches or pauses in its progress. Yet another technique – the most straightforward and unsophisticated by far – involves an indicator, something highly buoyant fixed to the line. If it's floating, there's no fish. If it disappears . . . well, there might be.

I took the easy option. I was learning, after all. I clipped a little lump of fluorescent styrofoam to my leader, and tried to quiet the voices in my head. *That's not fly fishing,* they told me. *That's cheating.* I didn't entirely disagree with those voices. This was not quite fly fishing as I'd previously known it. But an indicator was a safe and simple way to start. It was an aid to learning, like a child's inflatable armbands when they first begin to swim – and pretty much the same colour, too.

A lot of casting is involved in this technique. Or, more accurately, flicking or flipping, since there wasn't really the space in which to cast, and since line drag cannot be avoided at long distances. Six metres or so was as far as I needed to reach, then the little orange indicator would gallop back towards me, like a tiny puppy, eager to please. Flip, gallop, lift, repeat: that was the routine. Once, the styrofoam disappeared, and I lifted the rod tip, but nothing was there. The second time it happened, I was attached to something solid, a stone or a log. This was a common problem, I would come to learn. The line snapped, and I tied on another fly.

I moved farther downstream, following a fence alongside a sheep field, ducking beneath overhanging branches. There was debris from the flood everywhere, tangles of vegetation, broken branches, plastic. I was having to stoop beneath trees, pushing brambles aside to avoid piercing my waders, then fighting my way through thick stands of sweet-stinking Himalayan balsam. I found another spot, slid gracelessly off the bank, into deeper water than I'd expected, then took a few steps towards the middle of the river. A dipper perched on the opposite bank and sang to me. The melody was composed of metallic squeaks, sampled into a song, with a disgruntled, territorial tone. The bird fluttered upstream, then a few minutes later it passed me again, going in the opposite direction. It left me with only the sound of the river.

I started again: flip, gallop, lift, flip, gallop, lift. The repetition was hypnotic. So too was the indicator, a minuscule thing in the universe towards which all of my attention was directed. I remember this from my earliest years of angling, when much of the fishing I did involved floats. You watch them with an attentiveness unlike almost any other. You *see* and *see* and *see*, in taut antici-pation of *not seeing.*

Each time the little piece of foam went under I would lift the rod expectantly. Eighteen times out of twenty, it was nothing. On the nineteenth, I caught the riverbed, and lost another fly. On the twentieth: a fluttering little trout, no more than five inches long, which leapt and danced and then was gone. Five minutes later, I hooked another, identical in size.

I flicked the flies a few feet farther, letting them drift beneath the trees on the other side. It looked a perfect spot, where something larger might be hiding. But noth-ing happened. I flicked again, and the tail fly clamped itself to a branch. I tugged hard and the line snapped. I tied another, then continued, until I hooked another branch. This time, I lost both flies. I tied another tippet on, pulled the knots tight and the line snapped. I did it again, and this time the whole lot slipped from my hand and coiled around itself in a way I couldn't even begin to comprehend, and tangled so badly that, after several minutes of trying and failing to loosen it, I cut the whole lot off and began again.

I remember this feeling too, from thirty years ago: the feeling that so much can go wrong, that so many things lie between you and the fish. Mistakes, accidents, broken line, bad knots, leaking waders, flies that fall apart, flies that stick in trees or on rocks or in your clothes. I remember the months of teaching myself to fly fish, of failing to cast properly or to catch anything, of feeling, time after time, that I might as well give up, that I might as well go and sit beside the road and wait for my mother to come and collect me. Except, I never did give up. Not then.

I tied the tippet once more, solid this time. I turned and cast, back towards the bank, overshot and hooked a stem of Himalayan balsam. I waded over to retrieve the flies, bit them off the line and packed up. I'd had enough. I was ready to go home.

SECOND VISIT

A little farther downstream, near Tillicoultry, on a day that swung wildly between sunshine and rain. A week had passed and the water, while not quite clear, was considerably less turbid than before. The problems continued, though. The endless tangles; the line coiled, snapped and replaced; flies lost in bushes and in trees and on underwater snags; my feet sunk in silt, toppling me into the bank.

Then, in a deep, dawdling pool, entirely shaded by

trees, the indicator jolted out of sight. I struck, and felt the sharp struggle of a fish. It jerked a coil of line from between my fingers and held well down, shaking its head in the current. I tried to steer it towards me, cautious, fearing the line might snap, and feeling each unseen movement of its body. When it came, eventually, to the net, it was a brown trout of about a pound and three-quarters – though it had felt much larger. It was one of the most perfect fish I have ever seen, broad-backed and heavily freckled, each big black spot haloed in white.

As I slipped the trout back into the river and watched it flinch and dart for cover, I laughed out loud with sheer astonishment. No skill of my own had led this fish to me. It was pure beginner's luck.

THIRD VISIT

In my early years at high school, I would spend some of my lunchtimes in the library, leafing through copies of *Trout and Salmon* magazine. It wasn't the most popular publication they had in stock, by any means, so when a new issue arrived I was usually able to grab it. I read the articles first, and looked at the pictures. But I also spent a lot of time browsing the back half, the adverts for rods, reels and line. I had little idea what most of this stuff might be like, since I could only afford the very cheapest, nastiest of equipment, but I enjoyed learning the company names, looking at the prices, and imagining that one day I would be able to afford whatever fishing tackle I fancied.

As it turns out, that day never quite came. I do now have a little more expendable income than I had when I was thirteen, and I do still like to browse through the adverts and check out what, in a very different world, I could own. But most of it still feels entirely out of reach, aspirational rather than optional.

Having decided to continue my self-education in heavy-headed nymphs, however, I knew I would need another rod. The one I'd been using was too short and cumbersome to do what was required. It could neither hold the line up off the surface effectively, nor did it have the sensitivity to feel gentle, unseen takes. If I was to progress beyond the styrofoam indicator method – my little orange armband – I needed something else.

I followed my usual process for acquiring fishing tackle: I researched the subject extensively, looked at every possible option, then bought the cheapest appropriate rod I could find. Second-hand.

The whole set-up was even more unfamiliar now. I replaced the indicator with a French-style leader, long and tapered, with a two-foot section of colourful line just above the tippet. It was a nightmare to cast. The whip-thin, ten-foot rod, combined with the ultra-long leader, entirely undermined my previous sense of aerodynamics. Where standard fly casting uses the extended weight of the thick fly line to carry the flies outwards, with this technique there essentially *is* no fly line, just thin, light nylon. The only weight available is in the flies themselves, right at the very end of everything. Muscle memory, which would usually help guide my arm through each cast, was entirely useless. What I thought I could do, I could not. It was disorientating, like trying to ride a bike while wearing stilts. For the time being, even the most basic operation, getting the flies into the water, took effort.

The forecast had said cloudy, but the sun was blazing on the back of my neck as I stepped into the river, threatening to leave me burnt. Autumn was arriving, though, and the leaves were just beginning to turn from their summer softness to something more brittle, more frail. Jackdaws and rooks chattered in the trees and fields beyond the banks, and the air was thick with the smell of slurry.

I saw nothing at all in the first hour and a half of fishing, which was neither surprising nor particularly disappointing. At that stage, each cast that landed true felt like a success, and I watched the colourful line drift downwards with the sense that my job was already done, and that no further action was necessary. I trotted the flies through a few stretches where I thought, maybe, there might be fish, and I caught nothing. But then, in a swirling eddy where the line began to spin around itself, I lifted the rod tip and found a little trout attached. Two more came soon after. One mark of the unskilled angler is to always be surprised by fish, to never quite know when to expect them, or to expect them at incorrect times. That was where I was: flicking the flies almost randomly; then, when I had a hunch about what to do, getting it completely wrong.

The rain came on, almost without warning, so I packed

up and walked towards the car. Almost there, I stopped. On a branch above the river, a kingfisher was sitting, its feathers fluffed up against the weather. Usually, these birds appear as a flash of colour, a meteor of iridescent blue above the water. They hardly seem whole that way, just glimpsed, near-imagined. This one, though, was close to still, turning only its head, one way then the other, waiting for a break in the rain. I watched, drenched, until it gave up waiting, its little wings purring into brilliant flight.

FOURTH VISIT

Two days later and a couple of miles west. The river was slower here, and in the shallower pools were banners of weed swaying lazily in the current. I kept walking, looking for the deeper, faster corridors, the shadowy stretches, the places where food, shelter and oxygen should be plentiful.

I fished upstream, until I reached the edge of what appeared to be a shopping centre car park, where I turned around and fished down again. I was trying my best to be careful and attentive, to think about where I was casting and to fish with focus. I was trying to teach myself the semaphore of that fluorescent line, and the morse code of the fly on the riverbed, the tap-tapping of it, transmitted to my fingers.

It was, in all, a very different experience from my usual form of fishing. Like listening to a song in a language in which I'm not yet fully fluent, I felt as though I was always straining, reaching for something just beyond my grasp. I couldn't relax, because to do so would be to get everything wrong. And though the river was more familiar to me then than it had been when I first visited, that growing acquaintance could easily mislead. Many times, I thought I knew something that I really didn't.

I waded through one pool, where the water ran deep at the opposite bank, and at each moment I expected a take. When it didn't come, I tried again, and this time a tiny trout came wriggling into the net, four inches from nose to tail. I felt certain there were bigger fish there, but I couldn't find them.

At the lower end of another pool, where the river tightened into a swift bottleneck, I caught one fish, then another, then another, all of them between four and six inches long. I took a step upstream, let the flies cover the same water repeatedly, cast close to me, then in the middle, then the far side, just twelve or fifteen feet away. Another fish appeared, and another, each as little as the last. There must have been a shoal of them in there, packed tight, like the house martins that were flocking above me that evening, getting ready to migrate.

FIFTH VISIT

I walked from the car downstream, to where a herd of thirty young cows were relaxing on both banks. The animals watched me approach, then stood as one, waiting to see what I was going to do. I slowed, but continued. I am not ordinarily afraid of cows, but something in the demeanour of these animals made me hesitate. They looked bored, well fed, and gazed at me as though I might be about to provide them with some entertainment. They had that restless manner, like a gang of teenagers desperate for an excuse to misbehave.

When I stopped, the cows moved towards me – slowly, and not with obvious aggression. But there was enough certainty and speed in their steps to make me reconsider my options. They kept coming, and those on the opposite bank began to step in the river and cross. I was unnerved then. I had no desire to meet these animals head-on, and no faith that they were going to back down. So I looked for an alternative route.

The obvious exit was to one side, where I could hop a fence and be out of their way. But to do so would require getting into the river, and in the flow between me and that fence was a pair of swans with three cygnets. Unlike the cows, which were only a *potential* danger, the swans were a certain one. I looked at them and they looked at me. I could see it in their eyes; they were only too willing to break my arm.

I had to make a decision fast, so I turned around and went back the way I came. Really, I ought to have walked to the car and headed home. I should have taken all of this as a sign. But instead, I found a footpath by the road and followed it west, until I was far beyond where the cows had been standing. Then I crossed back into another field and made my way to the water.

I fished the pool where, a couple of weeks earlier, I'd

caught my one large trout, and this time I saw nothing. I fished the next pool up and saw nothing there either. I lost four flies, then another two. I spent precious time untangling, cutting and retying my line.

Is it possible, I wondered to myself, that I'm getting worse at this?

For the first time, I seriously considered that this technique might just not be for me. That I might be temperamentally unsuited to it. It seemed plausible, then. This kind of frustration is usually assuaged in angling by the fish that arrive, just often enough – the fish that are persuaded by what you do right, not the ones that are caught despite everything you do wrong. There is a subtle difference, but anglers know where the line between them lies. Deep down, they always know.

I caught two tiny trout in the end, when I'd almost given up, and I allowed myself a moment of self-reassurance. Perhaps this river is overfished, I thought, or perhaps too few trout are returned alive. It was notable that all but one of those I'd caught so far had been less than seven inches long. And if most of the bigger fish were getting knocked on the head, I surmised, that might explain my failure.

Or perhaps I was just making excuses.

SIXTH VISIT

I started at the same place where I had parked the very first time, a little way east of Dollar. As I put my waders on, and threaded line through the rod, two jays were screeching at each other in the branches above me, their disagreement evidently serious. I left them to it and walked down to the river. This time, the water was shallower, slower, clearer – almost unrecognizable, in fact, from that initial visit.

This would be, I guessed, the last time I would come to the Devon this year. Though there were still two weeks of the brown trout season left, I was feeling deflated. I was not getting to grips with the river, I thought, or with the techniques I was trying to learn. This form of angling seemed so much more difficult than what I was used to, with frustration and waste – of flies, line and time – apparently unavoidable.

I would give it one more go, I thought, then pack my things up for the winter.

On this stretch, upstream from the bridge, there was no path along the banks to follow. The land was steep and heavily wooded on both sides, making access difficult. The only way to make progress was to get in the water and wade. From above, leaves were falling, a light rain of red and gold and brown, slipping into the river and drifting away, upturned like cupped hands, carrying the season with them. I found footholds among the stones and gravel, and made my way in the opposite direction, casting when I could.

In a wide, riffled pool, the line stopped, and a fish of half a pound jumped twice then came sliding to my hand. In six visits, this was the second-largest trout that I had caught. Relief flooded through me as I turned the hook from its mouth, felt the tensing of its body in my hand, then watched it vanish back into the shadowed water. A little farther up, in a longer, deeper pool, I flicked the flies close to a fallen tree, where they paused almost immediately. I lifted the rod, assuming I was stuck on a submerged branch, but again I was attached to a fish, this one bigger still. It flashed deep, held itself hard in the current, then came to the net without further fuss – a golden, glorious thing.

From there, the river's banks seemed to close more tightly, into a narrow gorge crowded with trees. The sky above was blue, but the light was held at bay by the lattice of branches. I felt enclosed, almost claustrophobic, and in places steep stone cliffs rose straight from the water, making it impossible to even step on dry land. I was caught, for those moments, inside the river.

I reached a series of wide yet shallow waterfalls, like an enormous flight of steps, curving round and out of sight. Beneath the first of these was a deep pool, in which I felt certain there must be fish. But I couldn't find them. I cast and cast and cast, but nothing took. Here, a bigger, flashier fly might have made the difference. But I didn't have such a thing.

I waded over to one side of the rock face, where it looked possible to scramble up to the next level. I held the rod in one hand, stepped out on to a ledge, and with my other hand reached for a branch to give support as I shifted my weight. The branch came immediately towards me, unattached to any tree. I felt myself falling, took a step back for steadiness, but my foot met nothing, only air, and I kept going, backwards, downwards, into the water. I had no time to think or to control my fall, so it was something close to a miracle that I landed upright, the water not quite over the top of my waders, with the rod still in my right hand and the little rucksack still on my back. A rock was wedged deep into my left leg – a bruise-to-be that would spread over the coming days – and I felt a sharp pain rising in that side. I hauled myself out as fast as I could, shaken by the suddenness of my fall and by my utter inability to prevent it.

I felt newly vulnerable then, and I moved more cautiously, my heart slowing as I stepped up and away from the water, then higher, to where the rock flattened out again, and the river braided through cracks and deep gashes before its plunge. The pool at this second level was much narrower than the one below, but the fish were there. They came up to the flies with a kind of desperation, nipping at them without grabbing hold. I could see the flash of their bodies, turning in the cold current, and eventually one took hard enough to be hooked. Ten inches in length, it seemed a remarkable fish for this tiny space, and I wondered how long it could cling to this pool before being washed down into the deeper one below.

I tried to find a way up to the next level, but quickly changed my mind. I stepped, then slipped, into water that was too fast for comfort. Sopping moss offered no purchase when I tried to steady myself, and it wasn't worth the risk of continuing. Instead, I turned around and clambered back to the lower part of the river. I began walking, then striding downstream, allowing the current to stretch each step.

I passed the places in which, not long before, I had caught fish, but kept going until I was nearly back at the bridge. I paused, then, beside a throat of deep water that I hadn't noticed earlier. The river was wide there, but close to one bank the flow squeezed between a pair of boulders, where food would be funnelled. I cast to that spot between the rocks, let the fly be carried down, and a little fish was there. I lifted it quickly from the water, and on instinct cast back to the same place. This time, the resistance was much more solid, and the trout rushed downstream, using the current against me. I turned and felt a shudder of excitement as the rod bent towards the water. I tightened the line on the reel and led the fish gently up into the waiting net. Once again, I was laughing.

The downside to allowing myself to become a beginner again was the humiliating sense that what ought to be easy was not, that a skill I had spent years learning had been almost entirely *un*learned. The upside, though, was this: a revival of that thrill with which my early years of angling were infused, the feeling that a fish on the line, in the net, in the hand, was a kind of miracle. My capacity for amazement had been renewed.

I held the trout with its head facing upstream, let the water rush through its gills, and then opened my fingers. It shivered into life, with a flick of its whole body, and surged back into the space in which I'd found it. Invisible again.

IN THE WAY
OF WILDNESS

I'M STANDING ON A LITTLE wooden jetty, casting
flies into an oversized pond, a hole in the ground, stuffed
full of trout. It's a fishery not far from where I live, but it
could be almost anywhere. There are hundreds of places
like this across the United Kingdom, and thousands
more beyond. I've visited half a dozen or so in my years
of angling, and none of them really stand out. Even
where efforts have been made to naturalize the surroundings, with trees and shrubs growing at intervals
along the bank, and woodland blocking out the world
beyond, there is never any escaping the artificiality of
such places. The grass is neatly mowed; the designated
fishing spots are marked and numbered; the trout are
delivered from a hatchery at regular intervals.

I see the first of these fish just as I arrive: a rainbow trout, finning in the shallows beneath the platform. It's clearly struggling, with a wide white band of fungal growth along its flank and tail. It may have been injured en route from the hatchery, or by an incompetent angler. There are strict rules here about returning fish safely and quickly – if returning them is what you wish to do – but not everyone does a good job of that. One man, just up the bank from me, leaves a trout thrashing in the landing net for several minutes before slipping it back. This kind of mishandling can scrape slime from a fish's body, leaving it vulnerable to infection.

For many fly fishers, a place like this is where all of their angling is done, and the appeal, I suppose, is obvious. The regular stocking means that catching fish, while not quite guaranteed, is at least highly likely, and the average size of those fish is much larger than it would be elsewhere. If you want to take home trout to eat, this is the perfect place to go. It's also a sociable place, if you want it to be, and at least half of the visitors on this day are here in pairs or groups of three. They net each other's catches, they take photographs, they congratulate each other – and themselves.

The very first trout I caught came from a fishery, somewhere in the south of England. It was much smaller than this one – an old mill pond, if I remember right – and its fish were even more tightly packed, their numbers kept high in order not to test children's patience too far. Back then, it was a treat to be able to catch these creatures and eat them, too. Now though, I'm less certain. I visit one a couple of times a year at most, and nearly always when the brown trout season is closed, meaning other options are limited. I go when desperation strikes, when the eagerness to cast outweighs all nagging reservations.

Persistent as they are, those reservations are quite tricky to pin down. To sneer at this kind of angling, with its synthetic surroundings and flabby rainbow trout, is to risk sounding like an elitist, a tweed-trousered snob. Which is odd when you think about it. After all, this is hardly an inexpensive way of catching fish. For the price of six hours at this lake, I can get a year's angling on a nearby river. That's right, a *year*. So while I'm sensitive to accusations of elitism, in this case I don't quite buy it.

There are many differences between the fish in this pond and the fish in that nearby river. The river holds wild, native brown trout, whereas these are mostly rainbows, which are native to the western United States. They are also mutants, these fish – 'triploids', as they're known – with three sets of chromosomes instead of two. This mutation is achieved by applying heat or pressure to eggs in a hatchery, and its purpose is to render the resulting fish infertile. Nearly all stocked trout in the UK, and especially non-natives like these, must by law be unable to reproduce. This prevents them from interbreeding with wild fish, or from spreading, in case of an escape.

The biggest difference, though, between the trout cruising in front of me and the ones I try to catch elsewhere, is that, despite their superficial resemblance to wild creatures, these fish, in terms of their life experience, are more akin to products. They are animate meat, whose one reason for being is to be bought and sold. Most will live no more than a few days or even hours in this lake, having spent the rest of their lives in a hatchery or fish farm. In another fishery, not far from this one, I once watched an angler cast to the spot where trout were being poured in from the back of a tractor. He caught one immediately – the fish arrived hungry – and looked mighty pleased with himself as he knocked it on the head. The trout had only a minute of freedom in its entire life.

It's a funny enterprise this, like hunting cows in a field (or, let's be frank, like shooting pheasants). I tell myself that by returning these fish alive, as I tend to do, I am committing some droll act of dissent. But if I am, it's not a very good one. In reality, I'm just saving the owners some money while wasting my own.

There are good reasons, it must be said, to defend little fisheries like this. For one thing, they provide accessible angling throughout the year, and the near-guarantee of trout that are often big enough to feed a family. For another, they take pressure off wild fish populations, and away from places that could not sustain this level of angling traffic. But I can't shake the feeling that there is something ugly, even sordid, about this set-up, something that grates against everything I love most about fishing.

When I was young, each and every fish I caught felt like an expansion of the world, a secret I alone had uncovered. Mostly, it still feels like that. A trout, conjured into existence on the end of my line, is one of the most remarkable, thrilling things I know. But that magic trick does not delight me here. Not any more. These are fish that have no secrets, fish whose lives are priced, plotted and delimited by human beings, whose very DNA is remoulded for the benefit of anglers. Catching them seems to me to offer no expansion and no revelation. Some days – and this is one – it can feel like the opposite: a trick with all the wonder stripped away.

Angling is a way of exploring. It offers access to places and to living things that are ordinarily hidden from human eyes. Every cast is a reaching out, an extension of the self, into an underwater realm from which we spend most of our lives divided. This reaching out is both a physical and, just as importantly, a cognitive act. It is about attention, about the way one's thoughts and questions are directed towards the water, the *particular* water, in which one is fishing.

It would be possible to fish the same river, the same lake, the same pond, for a lifetime, and always be learning, always be conscious that there are things left to be disclosed. With each visit, each cast, the water would grow larger and clearer, magnified by an endlessly replenishing sense of curiosity and care. (That's not a bad definition of love, when you think about it.) But for most anglers, thoughts wander, and part of the pleasure they find in fishing comes from directing their attention towards new places, from exploring in a more literal way.

To set out for new water, to fish rivers, lakes and oceans for the first time, can be enormously exciting, even if that water is just up the road – a hidden stream you hadn't previously known was there. Where fishing is concerned, a sense of discovery and adventure is kindled with ease, and is heightened, I think, by the urge to connect with what is un-human or 'wild'. For Harry Middleton – one of the most distinctively lyrical of angling writers – that urge was central to his obsession with fishing in secluded mountain rivers. He was driven, he wrote, by 'the deep ache to be joined again, even if for a passing moment, to the natural world, that past of life in which everything is whole and united, mountains and rivers, trout and human beings'.

For many who fish, the excitement of exploration can be amplified even further by distance and by novelty. A whole travel industry has developed to cater for restless anglers. Those who have enough money lying around can hop on a plane to catch bonefish in the Bahamas, or Chinook salmon in Alaska, or golden mahseer in the mountains of Nepal. The appeal of such trips is partly about fish, of course, about catching what cannot be caught at home. But it is no less about place.

It's hardly surprising then that so much angling literature – at least the part of it that's not concerned with instruction – is impossible to fully disentangle from travel writing. There are authors for whom deep acquaintance with 'home water' is their primary subject, and the most skilled of them succeed in illuminating their places in a way that only the richest writing can do. For others, however, variety is key.

When I was eleven or twelve, I found a copy of Negley

Farson's *Going Fishing* in the public library in Lerwick. Published in 1942, fifty years before I picked it up, it is one of the classics of this genre – a real angling adventure story. The library kept a copy, I assume, because it contained a chapter about fishing in Shetland, and it was to that chapter that I turned first of all. 'For sheer grandeur I doubt if there is anywhere a more magnificent part of the world than you will find in the Shetlands [sic]', wrote Farson, in characteristically gushing style. 'Sea trout caught in the salt estuaries or in those peaty burns, or brown trout taken among the granite ledges of the windy lochs, will provide you with memories with which you can invigorate yourself for the rest of your life.'

It was exhilarating stuff, and when I'd finished that chapter, I went back and started from the beginning of the book. The USA, British Columbia, South America, Russia, Norway and what then was Yugoslavia: Farson criss-crossed the globe. He wrote of a stream in England where 'you will fish all day with a cast so fine that it looks like a strand of a brunette's hair', and of a river in Chile where trout under five pounds are thrown back for being too small. I turned the pages compulsively.

Negley Farson's restlessness had its roots in an unsettled and unpredictable childhood. From the start, angling was a means of escape: 'the further away from home it was', he once wrote, 'the better it would be'. Later, that restlessness found the perfect outlet in his job as foreign correspondent for the *Chicago Daily News*, a role at which he excelled. Farson had a particular talent for being in the right place at the right time. He was in St Petersburg (or

Petrograd, as it was then) when the Russian Revolution broke out. He interviewed Gandhi and saw him arrested by the British. He was in the Irish parliament the night they voted to abolish the pledge of allegiance to King George V. He watched both Lenin and Stalin make speeches. He met Hitler, Franklin D. Roosevelt and Ramsay MacDonald. He drank with F. Scott Fitzgerald and out-drank Ernest Hemingway. He witnessed some of the most dramatic events of the early twentieth century. And he found solace and adventure in angling.*

Negley Farson was part of the first generation that could globetrot at any real pace, and *Going Fishing* provided a

---

* In the summer of 1997, I was on a train from London, heading to the Glastonbury Festival with a friend. The two of us sat down together at a table, where we were joined by a well-dressed and well-spoken old man who seemed eager for company. I remember someone not yet drunk but working on it. A bottle of champagne stood on the table between us and was steadily emptied as the train moved westward. Between Paddington and Castle Cary the man regaled us with stories of people and places we knew nothing or little about: of Francis Bacon, the artist, with whom he had been friends, and of Soho in the 1950s. We listened, too ignorant to say or ask much meaningful in return. But the man seemed glad to have an audience, and for the length of that journey we were glad to be it.

It was not until five months later, when I saw his photograph alongside an obituary in the newspaper, that I learned who this man had been. Daniel Farson: prolific author and television presenter. And it was not until several years later, when I read Negley's memoir, *The Way of a Transgressor*, that I made the connection between father and son.

Both men, it turned out, drank themselves to death.

model for many of the angling writers who came after him. But travellers had been fish-seeking for a long time before Farson set out. In fact, that model of the footloose fisherman is in part a colonial one, rooted in Europe's history of international pillaging. Wherever the British and other imperial powers went in the world, there would always be some among them who carried rods. They explored the water, just as they explored and terrorized the land.

What is curious though – and typical of the whole imperial enterprise – is that these early expeditionary anglers were never really content with what they found elsewhere. Not for long, anyway. I suppose it shouldn't be surprising that colonists with a deep-seated conviction in the superiority of their own culture should extend that conviction even to the aquatic. For that is what they did. The fishes of the world were not good enough for anglers at the far reaches of the empires, and so, as soon as the technology made it possible, they brought their own along with them.

Carp were among the first species to be transported, and are now considered an invasive pest in some parts of the world. But the most common fish to be shipped out from Europe to the colonies in the nineteenth century were brown trout. Any region in which they did not already live was seen as an opportunity, a space waiting to be filled. Trout, farmed and stocked, could provide both sport and food.

The first successful transportation of brown trout eggs was from England to Australia in 1864. Of the 2,700 fertilized ova packed on to the clipper *Norfolk*, between layers of moss and ice, only 300 were still alive by the time they reached Melbourne almost three months later. But 300 was enough. From there, the fish were distributed into lakes and rivers in southern Australia and Tasmania, and then, in 1867, to New Zealand. The globalization of *Salmo trutta* had begun. (In contrast, the trout's big cousin, the Atlantic salmon, proved entirely unsuitable for live export. Over 100,000 salmon eggs were carried on the very same voyage as those first trout destined for the Antipodes. Once released, however, they headed out to the ocean and were never seen again.)

Brown trout thrive in cold water, which imposes some geographical limits on their success. But as the nineteenth century turned towards the twentieth, suitable habitat was located for them in countries across the world. They were brought to Canada in 1883, to South Africa in 1890, to Kashmir in 1900, to Kenya in 1905, to Argentina in 1909. Anywhere they *might* survive, they were given the chance to try. Today, they occupy every continent on earth, apart from Antarctica. Their presence has caused havoc within ecosystems the world over – putting many native fish species under threat – and yet, because they are so prized by anglers, because they bring visitors and money along with them, this damage is to a great extent overlooked.

The first brown trout to be taken to the United States were brought from Germany to New York in 1883, with another shipment arriving two years later, from Loch Leven, in Scotland. They were stocked, and quickly spread, with self-sustaining populations now present in the majority of states. As far as anglers were concerned, this was a great success. But unlike most of the countries to which these fish were brought, the US already had numerous trout species of its own. According to current taxonomical wisdom, there are three in the genus *Oncorhynchus* that are native to the United States: rainbow and cutthroat trout, both of which have multiple subspecies, and the Gila trout (a subspecies of which, the Apache, is sometimes described as a species of its own). In addition, there are five species in the genus *Salvelinus*, the char family: brook trout, lake trout, bull trout and Dolly Varden. A possible fifth species, the silver trout, is now extinct. The US didn't really need another trout, but they got one anyway. Old World nostalgia made it so.

Around the same time that brown trout eggs were being pressed into boxes of moss and shipped around the globe, one of those species that were native to North America began to make voyages of its own. Rainbow trout, originally found only in the far west of the country, had become a popular fish with anglers. They were more aggressive than brown trout, and therefore somewhat easier to catch. They were beautiful, grew large and fast, and tasted good. They were also vigorous, and could withstand higher water temperatures than other species. In all, rainbows seemed to be a perfect fish for breeding and for stocking.

They came by train, the first of them: 500 eggs, packed in much the same manner as their European counterparts, rumbled on the rails between California and New

York in 1875. These were the pioneers, the trailblazers, but their journey was soon eclipsed by others. Within a decade, there were rainbow trout in almost every state in the union. And further afield, as well. These upstart Americans were already making their way to Europe. It was a rapid expansion in territory, fuelled by fishermen's enthusiasm for the species.

Anglers these days like to pat themselves on the back for their environmental awareness. Aquatic ecosystems go largely unnoticed by most people, and responsibility for protecting those ecosystems has often fallen to those individuals who enjoy standing knee-deep in the water. Fishing clubs and associated campaigning groups, such as Trout Unlimited in the US, and Salmon and Trout Conservation in the UK, put pressure on local and national governments over issues such as pollution, habitat destruction and the ecological damage associated with salmon farming. They conduct extensive (and expensive) river restoration projects. And they do a lot of good.

But there is little room for smugness and self-congratulation. Terrible things have been done for the benefit of anglers – by state agencies as well as by anglers themselves – and much of it has happened because of our pickiness, our preference for certain species over others. When rainbow trout became the favoured fish for stocking, not just in the United States but worldwide, it was bad news for other species. Some were just out-competed, eaten or displaced by these big, silver bullies. Others were removed more directly. Hard as it may seem now to believe, entire river systems in the US not so long ago were deliberately poisoned, emptied of all fish, in order to make way for rainbows. In the 1950s and 1960s, the heyday of this madness, the US Fish and Wildlife Service poured tens of thousands of gallons of rotenone, a chemical that kills all fish and many aquatic insects, into rivers across the country. Hardly anyone back then even thought to question it.

In just over a century – between 1898 and 2006 – thirty-nine species of fish became extinct in North America, with another fifty-three to eighty-six species predicted to be gone by 2050. There is not always a single, identifiable cause for such vanishings (though 'human interference' pretty much covers it), but the flooding of waterways with large and aggressive alien species is undoubtedly one of the key factors in this loss.

It's not just the species anglers don't like that have suffered in this fervour for hatchery-bred fish, either. In the early 1970s, biologists in Montana made the counter-intuitive discovery that stocking rainbows did not actually increase the overall number of trout in a river. In fact, it did the opposite. The numbers dropped. It seems hard to credit: throw thousands of extra fish into a piece of water, and you end up with fewer than you started with. But it was right, and the reasons are not a mystery. Stocked fish are belligerent and ill-equipped for life outside a tank. On arrival in a river, they will attack and displace wild fish, thereby immediately damaging natural stocks. But in turn they themselves tend to die quickly. They waste energy, fail to catch food effectively, and get themselves killed by predators, both human and non-human. Those that do survive, and that manage to breed with other trout, will spawn a generation of fish that are not genetically adapted to their surroundings, and that therefore will also tend to be short-lived. 'Two plus two, in other words', as Anders Halverson has written of this phenomenon, 'often equals one.'

Montana followed the science. Their fisheries department ceased stocking rivers, and within just a few years catch rates began to soar. Today, the state is one of the foremost trout-angling destinations in the world, and over the intervening decades many other places have followed suit, with similar results. But the logic of this decision is still questioned by anglers and their representatives, in clubs and fisheries organizations. As an equation, *stock more = catch more* has the benefit of simplicity, even if it's not – in the long or even medium term – actually true.

Not so very long ago, almost every watershed held fish that had evolved to thrive in the distinctive conditions of that one place. There was, then, a remarkable degree of diversity between trout found in one river or lake and trout found in another: diversity of appearance, of behaviour, and of genetics. It was a kind of richness that we humans are not good at cherishing, and it tied these creatures – intimately, inextricably – to the places in which they lived. Fish, unique to their surroundings, were part of what made those surroundings, in turn, unique. And though it still exists in certain locations and to a certain extent, much of this diversity has been lost.

Rainbow trout were once limited to waters in the far west of North America and the far east of Russia. Within that one species were a host of subspecies, native to particular regions, and in some cases particular lakes and streams. Today, rainbow trout are present in at least eighty countries worldwide, and along with other stocked fish they have altered forever the waters in which they now live. Hatchery-reared trout are a genetic muddle, and regular interbreeding with wild fish means that many of those subspecies that previously existed, now, effectively, do not.

One of the ways of reducing the harm that stocked fish can cause has been the introduction of triploid trout, like the rainbows cruising around this pond in front of me. Unable to reproduce, their ability to damage ecosystems is at least limited to their own lifetime. And in a place like this, where the possibility of escape is virtually nil, and where there are no wild fish with which they can compete, they are, I guess, the perfect choice. But that doesn't mean I have to like them.

In trying to maximize the geographical range of those species that most appeal to us, and in failing to recognize or to value the ways in which fish and their places are entwined, anglers have created trout that are natives of nowhere. We have damaged many of the waters that we claim to love, and have made them more alike in the process. The result of our exploring, our wandering, our ecological meddling, is that one place is now less distinct from another than ever before. Seeking out that distinctiveness, that dwindling wildness that human actions have so imperilled, is now, for many anglers, a large part of why they choose to fish.

A text message arrived from my brother, with a map attached. It was a screenshot, a rectangle of land and water, cropped from a digital Ordnance Survey chart. The space it covered wasn't large – just two or three square miles at most – and it wasn't somewhere I knew. Or not precisely. Of the dozen or so names that were present on the map, I recognized only one of them for certain: a narrow Atlantic inlet at the north of the picture, which located it with some degree of specificity. But even without that clue, I'd have known that it was somewhere in Shetland. Just the look of the words, the juxtaposition of Norse and English names: it could hardly have been anywhere else.

Protruding from one side of this image was a little road, a track, which petered out in the space between the sea and a steep hillside. South and west of there, a hundred and fifty metres up the hill, were four small lochs, dotted unevenly around. Planted in one of them was a purple flag, a digital X to mark the spot.

I have fished in Shetland for thirty years now, on and off, and I had never heard of any of these lochs. Not once. Their names were entirely new to me. To some extent that's not so remarkable; there are at least five hundred lochs in the islands, and I've visited only a fraction of those. But I've spent a lot of time looking at maps, and a lot of time listening to anglers tell stories; and in all those years I'd neither noticed nor heard of these lochs.

What was particularly surprising, then, was the message behind the purple flag. It told me that this loch held treasure. The night before, my brother had been staying in the area, on a weekend break with his family. On a whim, once the children went to bed, he'd taken his fly rod and walked up the hill, and cast into the first water he found. Judging by the excited texts I received that night and the following morning – after he got up at 5 a.m. to go back a second time – this was a place that I really ought to have known about. There were big fish feeding in the margins, he said, cruising in stony, shallow water. He couldn't get them to take. Not that time. But they were there, and so he'd return.

Growing up in Shetland, fishing meant freedom. It meant being able to wander and explore and to stop at any loch you fancied and cast a fly. It meant a choice of waters that would take years, even decades, to exhaust. Of those five hundred lochs in the islands – nearly all of which hold trout – the vast majority are open to members of the local angling club. I know of only three or four, in fact, that are not.

This is how most of the fishing in my life has been done: with the great luxury of whim. I'm driving to a loch I last visited five years ago, and which, for reasons I can't explain, has been lately on my mind. But as I turn a corner, on the one-track road that will take me the last few miles, I see something else. I see a loch, not far from the road. It's a loch I have passed many times, but have never really noticed until now. And now I can't *help* but notice, for the surface is calm, and there are fish rising all over. Small fish, maybe, but it's hard to tell. I slow down, park the car beside a gate and get out. I set up the rod, then hop the fence.

To be able to do this, to have such a rich, expansive choice of places in which to fish, is a rare thing indeed. Rare in Scotland, rare in the UK, probably rare world-wide. Certainly, it's not like that where I live now. Here, almost every piece of water requires another fee, another membership. Some are affordable – and to those I am, by necessity, drawn. Others are considerably less so. Then, there are the private clubs, or 'syndicates', about which there is most often no information to be found online. Membership of these tends to be available by invitation only. I have never received such an invitation, and per-haps never will. I don't know the right kinds of people, and I don't know where to find them.

Inevitably, then, the freedom I once found in fishing has been curtailed since I left Shetland, and the ability to connect with place in this way has likewise been limited. Now, the degree of freedom that's available, and where it can be exercised, is dependent upon whom I know, and on the fullness or otherwise of my wallet. (Which is not unusual when it comes to freedom, I suppose.)

There is an irony to this, though, an irony that only adds to an angler's frustrations. For here in Scotland, we possess a kind of liberty that is both precious and yet, too often, taken for granted. There is a right to roam in this country, a right to walk and wander, responsibly, through both public and private land. It's a right that exists elsewhere in Europe – in the Nordic countries, for instance – but not in England, and certainly not in the United States.

But this right to roam exists alongside a distribution of land that is, frankly, grotesque. The historian Jim Hunter has claimed that Scotland possesses 'the most concentrated, most inequitable, most unreformed and most undemocratic land ownership system in the entire developed world'. Fewer than five hundred people own half of the private land in the country. Enormous estates – many of them belonging to landlords who live most of the year elsewhere – are run for the benefit of the very wealthy, who pay excruciating sums of money to holiday in the Highlands, to shoot stags and grouse, catch salmon and sip whisky.

I can walk across these estates if I want to. I can jump up and down and wave my arms around in sight of the lords and ladies and shipping magnates and tech billionaires for whom the land is a playground. It's not much compensation for the inequities of the system, but it's important nonetheless.

The problem here is essentially the exact opposite of the one faced today by American anglers. Here, I can walk the banks of pretty much any piece of water in the country. I can peer into its depths, and dip my toes beneath the surface. If I want to, I can swim. But in the vast majority of cases, I cannot cast a fly without paying someone for permission.

In the US, there is a great deal more water under public ownership, for which each state offers fishing licences. Furthermore, in many of those states *all* water is considered to be public property. Anglers there are presumed to have the right to fish, so long as they can gain access. Which is where the problem lies. Land-owners alongside that water can, and do, prevent people from reaching it. Trespassing laws are used to keep anglers out, and to make money from what is, in theory, a common good.

In Scotland, I can reach the water, but I can't always fish; in the US, you can fish, but you can't always reach the water.

For those seeking freedom and escape, there are still options. You can throw money at your hobby, if you've got it. You can fly to Florida and catch tarpon; or, better still, you can take the boat to Shetland. But there are other ways, too, and some anglers are now looking for adventure in precisely those places where it might seem least likely they would find it.

Matthew Miller, in *Fishing Through the Apocalypse*, has written that 'in a world where there are almost no unexplored, uninhabited places left, perhaps the post-industrial wastelands will become the new frontier. The places where the dreamers, the outcasts, the renegades, and those with low-grade utopian visions will go to escape the conformist world.'

For anglers, that new frontier is the antithesis of the places with which our sport has most often been associ-ated: the 'wild', the 'remote', the 'unexplored'. Today, if you're looking for exciting trout fishing, you may well find it closer to home, in towns and cities. The rivers that run through these urban spaces – which are where they are *because* of those rivers – were once filthy. Many were biologically dead. They were covered with concrete, banished to drains and culverts. They were ignored and forgotten. They were treated like sewers. But that's changing.

In an essay documenting his search for trout in the half-hidden streams and rivers of London, the writer and conservationist Charles Rangeley-Wilson – a literary descendant of Negley Farson if ever there was one – described his quest as being 'about looking for the edge: the edge of destruction, the edge of what is holding on'. What he means, I think, is this: Fishing has always been a way of joining the human to the non-human world. It is a means of extending, of reaching, from one into the other. To further that reach, anglers often choose to put themselves in the way of wildness. It is there, in undomesticated places, that we are most aware of that border, that edge, where one world melts into another.

The edge that Rangeley-Wilson is referring to, though, is not to be found by exploring outwards. Instead, it is moving in the other direction. It is the wildness that is now putting itself in the way of us. The restoration of urban rivers, supported, in the UK, by organizations like the Wild Trout Trust, is encouraging wildlife, including fish, to return to our towns and cities. That process of returning, of reclaiming, is a hugely important one. These are places that human beings poisoned, despoiled and disfigured, so unconcerned were we by the health of our surroundings. To see those surroundings now being clawed back, to see our damage being gradually undone, to see this 'edge of destruction' pushed tenaciously towards us, is really quite something.

Anglers are drawn to these recovering waters because the return of trout seems to prove something about the world. Something good. Something marvellous. Something hopeful. And what could be more freeing, more exhilarating, than that?

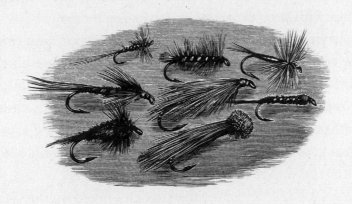

THE
RIVER DON

Aberdeenshire, 2015

IT WAS ALL WILL'S FAULT. Raising expectations to such heights meant the threat of disappointment loomed from the very beginning, a precipitous possibility on the edges of our vision. Driving to a quiet stretch of the River Don, he told me in detail about his previous visits to this piece of water. Never had he fished it without catching a trout of at least three pounds, he said. Not once.

I believed him then, and still do. Will is a good friend, not given to the kind of exaggeration in which some anglers specialize. But frankly, those stories set us up to fail.

All fishing requires a delicate balance of expectations, of confidence and optimism tempered by realism, by an acceptance that things don't always go your way. Stoic hopefulness, you might call it. Such a balance allows angling to remain enjoyable whether anything is caught or not. We wouldn't fish if there was no hope of catching; but nor would we fish if *not* catching felt like a disaster. Past successes can disturb that balance. Especially when the successes are not your own.

Will parked the car in the shade of overhanging trees, and we unpacked our gear from the boot, then walked along a field's edge towards the river. Halfway, we cut across, treading carefully in the ruts made by a tractor, trying our best to avoid the young crops. As we continued beneath a narrow stand of trees at the other side of the field, yellowhammers fizzled in song above us.

'This is a good place,' said Will, pausing some distance back from the bank. We knelt down and looked at the river.

It was a slow pool, perhaps thirty feet wide, fed by faster water above. The vegetation was tall and lush, but the banks were steep, so we could sit and watch without disturbing the fish.

'Okay, let's set up and see what happens.'

The pair of us stood, threading line through the eyes of the rods, then tying on tippets. Just a single hook was needed here, Will said.

'This is the one,' he told me, handing over a thin, curved fly, with a head of wispy duck's feathers that would hold it, hanging, in the surface film of the water.

'Cast this to a rising fish. They'll take it.'

So far, we had not actually *seen* a rising fish, but Will's confidence remained infectious. We decided to wait, and began with lunch. I opened a pack of sandwiches and lay back, trying to avoid the nettles and thistles that were lurking in the grass. The afternoon was not quite warm, but it was warm enough, in our waterproofs, to be comfortable. We didn't speak much, just ate our bread, then biscuits, then peanuts, and waited.

'Just a few more insects in the air and I reckon we'll start to see some fish,' Will said. 'Over near the opposite bank, where that run of bubbles is: that's a good spot.'

We kept watching.

Above the water, house martins and swallows wing-flitted, snatching bugs from the air, swooping and diving between the banks. Thirty yards farther upriver, a dipper was doing its thing, bouncing from a rock, midstream, into the water, under, then out again. The clouds were thinning. A brisk wind ruffled the surface.

It was ten minutes, or perhaps even a little more, before the absence of rises was specifically mentioned. Only one fish had splashed since we arrived, just downstream, but it was obvious from the sound of that disturbance that the trout was not worth standing up for.

'I'm pretty sure if we wait just a bit longer we'll start to see a few more flies hatching,' Will said. 'Then the fish'll come up. Casting at rises is definitely the best way to go.'

I waited a few more minutes, then pointed out, not too sharply, that there were already a lot of flies – that they were, in fact, swarming in front of us. There were flies literally everywhere.

'Yes,' Will said, finally letting his frustration show. 'I can see them.'

Around about then, I suspect, he was regretting the absolute confidence with which he had advertised this place to me, the certainty with which he had burdened our visit. Faced now with an entirely blank river, he was quietly panicking.

For me, however, there was no panic, only an impatience to get my line in the water. I decided not to wait any longer.

'I think I'll try a nymph,' I said, biting off the dry fly, which had so far remained entirely dry. I picked out a little goldhead with a body of hare's fur, something small, simple and unobtrusive. The choice was random, instinctive. I saw it in the box and it felt right. I tied it on.

Near the top of the pool I began to cast, flicking the line upstream then mending the slack as it drifted down towards me. There was a heavy current so the goldhead was moving fast, staying clear of obstructions. It was fishing fine enough, I thought, and I felt a glimmer of confidence again. Sooner or later a trout would come my way.

Will, meanwhile, had also given up waiting and had waded out to float his fly close to the opposite bank. Soon enough, I heard a splash and turned to see him lift and swing a fish of about four inches out of the water and into his hand. It wasn't much, but it was a good sign, surely. Maybe. We continued.

After half an hour or so without any further success, we decided to abandon the pool. It wasn't working, clearly – at least not yet – so we would leave it and try again later. We walked upstream, round a bend in the river, to where the water was faster, shallower. We began again.

The same result. We continued.

By the time we returned to where we'd started, a couple of hours had passed, and between us we'd caught two or three trout no bigger than sardines. Every bit of that initial confidence was gone. We had seen nothing to suggest that any bigger fish were feeding, or were even present in the river. Not a single substantial rise had been witnessed, not a single significant bite had been felt.

'Well,' I said, 'what are we going to do?'

Will looked at the water, searching for some kind of answer. 'There are deeper pools downstream,' he said. 'Let's try there. Maybe we'll have more luck.'

'Maybe,' I replied, though by that time I was consoling myself with the fact that it was Will, not me, who had paid for our day's fishing.

We walked together to the bottom of that first pool, and then on beyond the next. I stopped at the lower end of a third pool, in a space beside a tree at the water's edge. I was restricted there – I couldn't move far, upstream or down – but it seemed as good a spot as any in the circumstances.

Will continued walking, and was soon out of sight.

When hope fades, you don't fish well. You don't cast

with care, or think clearly about what you're doing. You don't look for signs of what you ought to do next. You fish mechanically, not imaginatively. A lack of hope, when fishing, will very often prove itself well founded.

But not always.

After a dozen casts across the pool, as the fly ended its drift just to my right, it stopped dead. Mostly when this happens the cause is a rock, or some other underwater obstruction, and for a second I felt something like gratitude for the wrench of excitement this rock had delivered. But the fly didn't stop for long. Instead, it started to move in the opposite direction. Slowly, grudgingly, at first, until it felt the resistance of the rod; then it moved faster.

It took me longer than usual to feel certain that what I had hooked was indeed a fish, and that it was, as it seemed to be, a large one. But that certainty came, as I reeled the slack line from my hand, with a kind of panic.

Such moments demand witnesses, and I shouted for Will. Once, twice, but with no reply. I pulled my phone from my pocket, tried to dial his number with one hand, while, with the other, trying to keep control of the trout. 'Er, could you come back please,' I said, when he answered. 'I've hooked a big fish, and I think I might need help.' I hung up before he had a chance to respond, and I stuffed the phone back in my jeans.

The fish by now had taken a lot of line from my reel, and was skulking somewhere at the other side of the river. It kept its head down, powering away from me, first to one end of the pool and then the other. Fortunately for me, it seemed unwilling to go farther.

Will arrived, panting, having run from his position downstream. He was carrying – I was relieved to see – a landing net. I hoped that we were going to need it, but the fragility of my line was now a real concern.

'If that's a trout, then it's the biggest trout I've ever seen!' Will exclaimed, when he saw the bend in the rod, saw the way the fish took line from me so easily, and, through his polarized glasses, saw the fish itself, holding down near the bed of the river.

Then it jumped, and we understood.

The River Don is famed for its excellent trout fishing, but it is also known for its salmon. Many of those salmon will come in from the sea somewhat later in the year – this was just past the middle of May – but some of them arrive in spring. There was no mistaking it. This was not a trout.

Catching salmon has always seemed to me a rather different business than catching trout. Where trout fishing is about convincing the fish that your fly equals food, salmon fishing is a more complicated, uncertain thing. After all, once they return to freshwater from the sea, salmon don't eat. From the moment they arrive in the river, they will digest no food at all.

Catching them, then, has always involved a certain kind of mystery. What instinct does one need to trigger in the fish, if not hunger? The assumption most anglers make is that irritation is at least part of it. Haul a big, brightly coloured fly past their nose and, with the sort of frustration one might expect from a creature that hasn't eaten in days, they lash out, using the only weapon at their disposal: their mouth. Traditional salmon flies are large and highly visible. They are provocative more than imitative.

Which makes it all the more surprising that a salmon should have grabbed hold of my fly, since it was neither large nor colourful. Perhaps the flash of the gold bead was enough to prompt the reflex snap of its jaws. Or perhaps the fly just happened to drift into the fish's face, a brush against its skin that triggered it to strike, without looking twice at the object of its anger.

Salmon are enigmatic, unpredictable fish. They are also extremely strong.

It was nearly fifteen minutes before I had any sign the fish was tiring. It allowed itself then to be pulled close to where Will was standing, thigh deep in the river, with a little landing net stretched out in front of him.

'Try and bring it in over my right shoulder, towards the net,' he yelled, his excitement no less apparent than my own.

'I don't think it's ready,' I replied. 'In fact, it's definitely not ready.'

Coming close, then seeing Will's shadow fall across the water, the fish turned and powered back out again, first down towards the riffles at the bottom of the pool, then up and across, close to the opposite bank. It stripped line off the reel and stripped my nerves until they felt taut and close to breaking. I could feel it stop midstream and shake its head, trying to rid itself of the thing that was causing it so much bother. Each time I felt those hard shivers come galloping up the line I expected it to succeed, to come free and to leave me standing there, as hopeless as I'd been twenty minutes earlier.

Finally, after several more runs and a heart-stopping leap, the salmon loosened its grip on the river and resigned itself, just about, to the strange force that was pulling it bankward. The head came up, then the long silver body, sliding across the surface towards the net. That net, designed as it was for trout up to a few pounds, was not a safe destination for the fish, and there was a tense moment as it tipped in, head first, and Will, with his other hand, grabbed the 'wrist' of its tail, which, along with half the body, was still protruding from the net. He launched himself up and on to the bank. And there it lay.

Salmon freshly arrived from the sea are often described as 'bars of silver'. But that description doesn't even begin to express what these fish look like. Silver, yes. But thunderstorm blue as well – a hefty stripe of it – with fat black spots across its sides. One or two sea lice were still fixed to its flank, the tell-tale evidence that it had not been long in the river.

I held it up for a photograph – the largest fish I had ever caught – with one hand behind its head and one in front of the tail. It was as long as my arm. I stepped down into the water and put its mouth towards the flow. I felt, I must admit, a twinge of guilt. This salmon had swum miles up the river, intending to carry out the most important business of its life. For more than fifteen minutes I had wasted its energy, because the light trout tackle I was using could not control it any faster. The fish was exhausted, and it took a long time to revive. I moved it gently back and forth, letting the current push through its gills, watching them pulse and bloat until, with a kick of the tail, it was ready to go.

We fished on for several more hours, catching half a dozen tiny trout but seeing nothing more substantial than that. As the afternoon turned towards the evening, we sat down in the long grass, enjoying the sunshine that just then had opened out. The water purred through a slight bend there, curling like cigarette smoke around broad boulders, tarrying close to the banks. Flies were hatching too – cirrus wisps of insects hovered low above the surface – and it seemed that everything was perfect, that finally we might get what we came here for: the big trout that Will had promised. But fishing has a way of breaking promises, of offering, instead, only surprise.

Somewhere nearby, a reed warbler was singing, and rooks squabbled in the trees across the water.

We didn't cast again that day.

PUTTING BACK
AND TAKING AWAY

I AM HOLDING IN MY hand a slim piece of polished wood, ten inches long and gently tapered, with a heavy brass tip at one end and a small cap at the other. Attached is a lanyard, just large enough to slip over my wrist. Looking carefully, I can see evidence of poor production: the hardened glue squeezed out from beneath the metal, the cap just slightly misaligned. Yet, despite these minor flaws, it is a beautiful object, as comfortable and comforting in the hand as a wave-smoothed stone. Like a pocketknife, it has the elegance of a simple tool, perfectly designed.

With my fingers wrapped around and my thumb pressed lightly against the wood, I feel the balance of it, the weight concentrated at the front end, where its purpose lies. In this case, the purpose is killing fish, and the tool, to anglers, is known as a priest. One or two sharp knocks to the head and a trout will stiffen and quiver, its nerves kicking hard against what has already been decided.

Swinging the priest into my hand, I feel the sting of it in my palm, and I am reminded that its job is a serious one. Angling, this tool insists, is not just a hobby or a sport. For the fish, at least, it is a matter of life and death.

These days, this priest lives mostly in a cupboard, hardly ever coming with me to the waterside. I rarely kill fish any more – only once or twice a season at most – and when I do, I'm as likely to use a rock or to break a neck with my fingers as I am to have this cosh to hand. I like to keep it though, even just at home. It seems important not to forget that it's there.

Over the past half-century and more, 'catch and release' fishing has grown in popularity, both in Europe and in North America. Most angling clubs and authorities impose strict limits on the number of fish that can be kept, and many require the use of barbless hooks, to reduce the damage caused to fish that are caught and returned.

Not so long ago, such rules would have been unimaginable. To read almost any angling book from Izaak Walton in the 1650s right up until the early twentieth century is to be faced with a catalogue of slaughter that would make most contemporary anglers wince. Every fish would be thrown in the creel or slung up on the bank, whether it was going to be eaten or not. Little thought was given to the sustainability of fish stocks, nor to the ethics of unlimited killing.

It was the former concern especially that led to a gradual change in behaviour, a move away from taking everything that was caught. In the US, where the most popular waters attract large numbers of anglers, unsustainable pressure on fish stocks has been a serious problem for a long time. And it's been resolved, in most places, by the simple act of restocking. For more than a hundred years, state game agencies have been pouring hatchery-grown fish into rivers and lakes, and anglers have been pulling them out again. It seemed to fix the numbers problem, at least.

Not everyone likes this put-and-take logic, however, and from an ecological perspective it leaves a lot to be desired. For those anglers who would rather catch wild fish than those reared inside a tank, then, there are really only two choices: either seek out waters where few other people go, or else put fish back, so they can live, breed and be caught again.

There is a particular satisfaction to catch-and-release angling, a thrill that comes when the fish in your hand kicks beneath the surface and disappears, back to where it came from. It's the satisfaction of knowing that a thing that brought you pleasure is still out there in the world, and that the place from which it came is not deprived of its presence. But that pleasure can too easily slip towards smugness, and a self-regard that is not deserved. Environmentally, certainly, catch and release is a good thing.

It helps to maintain fish stocks, and to minimize the need for stocking. But ethically, things are not quite so simple.

While my priest may stay at home most of the time, and while nearly all of what I catch now goes back alive, I cannot escape the moral gravity of angling. I cannot let myself off the hook so easily. For many critics, the whole business of angling is inherently and inescapably cruel. And those criticisms, I think, are worth taking seriously.

A doctored photograph shows a household pet with a hook piercing its lip. Beside it, a question: 'If you wouldn't do this to a dog, why do it to a fish?' The image comes courtesy of PETA (People for the Ethical Treatment of Animals), and typically for that organization it is both shocking and crudely sentimental at once. A cute animal is substituted for a non-cute one, and a splash of blood is thrown in for good measure.

But the question itself is more valid than it might at first appear. Asked differently it is certainly worthy of consideration. Jack Turner is a mountain guide and Zen Buddhist. He is also a former philosophy teacher and a former angler. In a conversation with the writer Ted Kerasote, Turner directly criticized catch-and-release fishing, with a rather more apt and reasonable comparison than the one made by PETA:

> . . . imagine using worms and flies to catch mountain bluebirds or pine grosbeaks, or maybe eagles and ospreys,

and hauling them around on fifty feet of line while they tried to get away. Then when you landed them, you'd release them. No one would tolerate that sort of thing with birds. But we will for fish because they're underwater, out of sight.

He has a point. For a long time, anglers avoided much moral scrutiny because the creatures they hunt are so rarely seen alive by non-anglers. Fish are neither particularly cute nor particularly visible. But the question of why such treatment is acceptable should not be so easily dodged.

If forced to answer, many anglers will resort to a stock response – fish don't feel pain – and until quite recently there was little scientific evidence to the contrary. But that's not the case any more. In 2003, biologists at the Roslin Institute and the University of Edinburgh, led by Dr Lynne Sneddon, began to publish the findings of their studies into rainbow trout, which suggested the conventional wisdom was false. Not only did the trout possess the physiological capability to experience and process pain, including nociceptor cells around their face and lips, they also displayed precisely the kind of behaviour one would expect from a creature that suffers.

Not all scientists accepted this conclusion, and the reports were criticized by some who felt the evidence for *conscious* pain in fish was still unconvincing. For one thing, fish do not possess a neocortex, the part of the brain on which human consciousness relies. James Rose, a zoologist at the University of Wyoming, was particularly scathing towards the Edinburgh biologists, arguing that 'neither their rationale nor their supporting evidence is compelling, much less neurologically feasible'.

These days, though, Professor Rose may be in a scientific minority, and for anglers who are honest with themselves that shouldn't be surprising. Anyone who has hooked a fish understands that a fish doesn't like being hooked. From the moment of connection, it will fight for its life. It will dash one way then the other; it will jump into the air and shake its head frantically; it will pull with every bit of strength it can muster. A hooked fish will show something so akin to fear and panic that to avoid such terms is verging on dishonesty. And to deny the possibility that pain is at the root of this panic is hard to justify.

Is it really unreasonable, then, to suggest that angling might be inherently sadistic, or at the very least morally indefensible? Like cockfighting and badger-baiting, it is an activity in which pleasure is derived from the mortal struggles of a creature that is, to some degree, sentient. Few people today, at least in Europe and North America, would hesitate to describe those blood sports as cruel, so why not this one?

A perfectly reasonable way to answer this question would be to point out that, so far as we know, a fish's capacity for suffering is probably less than a cockerel's, and certainly less than a badger's. And the researchers in Edinburgh did not dispute this. They were careful to avoid suggesting that fish feel pain in the same way that we or other mammals do, for their work proves no such thing. It is not possible, of course, to show scientifically how an animal experiences the world, but the fact that, on average, fish have the smallest brains of any vertebrate, in relation to their body size, means that any conscious experience they do have is likely to be limited. And the fact that an individual fish may occasionally be caught several times in a single day, without apparent ill-effects, implies that any suffering is probably very short-term.

A second defence is that, in the majority of cases, there are two possible outcomes for a fish that is hooked and landed: either it will be returned to the water, tired but basically unharmed, or else it will be swiftly killed for the purposes of eating. This is very different from the mutilation and slow death suffered by animals that are forced to fight for human entertainment.

In addition to this, many anglers seek to reduce the harm they cause even further. They use hooks without barbs to try and prevent physical damage to the fish. They will also insist on using strong line so the fight can be kept short, and any stress minimized. Doing so reduces the chance of line breakage, too, which can leave fish permanently impaled.

There is no doubt that a fish dislikes being hooked, but its short-term prospects are less morally problematic than those of the fighting cock, badger or bull. They are also less problematic, I would argue, than the treatment of animals on factory farms, where suffering is sometimes extreme and protracted, and the fate of fish caught in commercial nets or reared in tanks and cages.

To summarize this line of defence, then, one could argue that, in contrast to most blood sports and much of our meat production, fishing inflicts limited pain on a creature with limited capacity for suffering. For many, this defence will suffice. But not for everyone. And if I'm honest, not for me.

Any discussion about the ethics of angling is ultimately part of a much broader philosophical conversation, at the heart of which is a question: What moral responsibility do human beings have towards animals? It's hard to know how to begin thinking about a question like this one, and the easiest thing, therefore, is not to do so. That is the option that, I suspect, most people choose, at least when it comes to wild animals. Their welfare and well-being are considered only when consideration is unavoidable – after injuring a deer with a car, for instance, or when deciding which type of mousetrap to set.

One of the great strengths of angling, I think, is that it makes it difficult to ignore the issue of moral responsibility. To fish is to engage directly and continually with questions of harm, of how our behaviour impacts other species, and of what heed we ought to pay that impact. Those questions have not faded, for me, even after many years of fishing. They still feel worth asking, reconsidering and asking again.

I value doubt when it comes to such dilemmas. Moral certainty often grows from an unwillingness to think, and an ethical position that is never questioned can easily harden into complacency or self-righteousness. It is tricky, then, to outline my own defence of fishing in terms that are not adorned with caveats and qualifications. It is almost like missing the point. And it is tricky, also, to do so in a way that does not feel detached from the practice of angling. Ethics should be rooted in lived experience, I believe, not confined within the pages of a book. Fishing has shaped my thoughts on this subject over many years, and it continues to do so. Those thoughts remain fluid, unfinished, and pinning them down in words is both awkward and unsatisfying.

As a place to start, however, a kind of general rule or summarising principle, I suppose I would begin with something like this:

We should seek to cause no greater harm to animals than we might reasonably expect them to experience in the course of a life in which we had not intervened.

I like the flexibility of this particular framing. I like the wiggle room it offers. It takes as given that physical harm – including the possibility of predation – are part of the natural life of any animal, and ought to be understood as morally neutral. Human intervention, therefore, is problematic only when it causes harm beyond that which might be expected in our absence.

Despite its flexibility, this principle would have enormous consequences if it were to be taken seriously. It would mean an end, for instance, to intensive livestock farming and to much animal experimentation, though it would still allow small-scale, welfare-conscious agriculture. Angling would not be prohibited by such a rule, and nor would certain kinds of hunting. But a caveat is needed already.

I believe strongly that fishing, hunting, and indeed any human interaction with animals ought to be carried out in a sustainable way. It ought not to cause unnecessary or long-term harm to the ecosystems of which those animals are a part. For me, moral responsibility towards individual creatures cannot be meaningfully considered without also taking into account a wider ecological responsibility. Towards that end, I would add a second principle, framed no less hesitantly than the first:

We should seek to maintain or improve the health of ecosystems and of the natural world more widely.

This rule might be better expressed in the words of Aldo Leopold, whose book, *A Sand County Almanac,* is one of the founding texts of American ecology and conservation. Introducing his notion of a 'land ethic', Leopold wrote that 'A thing is right when it tends to preserve the integrity, stability, and beauty of the biotic community. It is wrong when it tends otherwise.' This proposition expands the moral gaze; it sees not just the trout but the river and the watershed, too.

These two principles, in combination, feel helpful to me. Both are versatile and somewhat malleable, yet adhering to them fully would not be easy. While neither can provide a right answer to every moral question, together they feel like a good place to start. They offer an ethical foundation, a piece of fertile ground on which to stand and think.

Yet, while these propositions to me seem sensible and meaningful, I am conscious that others would fervently disagree. And while I am glad that those who find angling to be morally unacceptable are still very much in a minority, I don't wish their opposition away. Angling is serious, and it deserves to be seriously questioned. It is important, I think, to be familiar with the arguments against it.

Many people today believe that hunting, fishing, meat production and animal testing are all morally indefensible. The philosophical roots of this belief go back several centuries, but it was not until the 1970s that the ideas really took hold. And *ideas*, plural, is correct here, because there are two main ethical theories commonly employed in support of vegetarianism and against animal exploitation. Those two theories – utilitarianism and animal rights – have much in common, but their logic is somewhat different.

Peter Singer's book *Animal Liberation* was published in 1975, and it remains the best-known work on this subject. Singer is a utilitarian. That is, he believes that the rightness or wrongness of an action can be determined by the consequences of that action. A right action has positive outcomes; a wrong one has negative outcomes. Singer's basic argument is that the justifications people have previously used to exclude animals from moral consideration are incorrect. They are based on the belief that human beings are somehow exceptional, that we differ from animals in morally significant ways. But in fact, he points out, we are not so different. Many animals are sentient; they can feel pain and they can suffer. And if an animal can suffer, we ought to take that suffering into account. Crucially, he argues, human beings should not place our own interests above those of an animal. We should not place our desire to eat a pig, for instance, over the interest that pig has in remaining alive.

Animal rights theorists see things a little differently. For them, the specific consequences of an action are not exactly the point. The point, instead, is the rights of the individual, which should not be infringed. Philosophers such as Tom Regan argue that animals – or at least some animals – possess those rights, just as humans do, and therefore we have an obligation to respect them. We must treat animals not 'merely as means' to our own ends, in Regan's words, but as beings with 'inherent value'.

There are important differences between the utilitarian and animal rights arguments. For one thing, the latter is stricter, since no weighing-up of consequences is involved. Utilitarians, for example, could justify some animal testing for medicine, if the results would save many lives. Tom Regan would allow no such thing. Rights are not a numbers game. They are absolute.

What ties these two theories together, though, besides their insistence on a change in our diet and behaviour, is

that both demand that human ethics be extended outwards to cover non-humans. In doing so, they appeal to
the same basic logic as the women's liberation and civil
rights movements. Namely, that to make ethical distinctions based on group membership is arbitrary and
wrong. Ethical distinctions based solely on gender or
race are arbitrary and wrong, therefore ethical distinctions based solely on species are likewise arbitrary and
wrong. Such distinctions have been labelled *speciesist*.

There is a clear and persuasive logic to this argument,
and it is easy to be carried along by it. Sentience and the
ability to feel pain do indeed feel more meaningful as
criteria for moral consideration than simply *being
human*. That's why killing a monkey is different from
killing a houseplant. The problem, though, is that, unlike
the examples of racism and sexism, the logic of anti-
speciesism is not absolute. It can only be taken so far.
Beyond a certain point it ceases to be persuasive and
instead becomes obviously objectionable. There are few
people, for instance, who would argue that, if forced to
make a choice between killing a human or killing a trout,
anyone should seriously consider the former option.

Adherence to the principle of anti-speciesism, then,
has to be qualified. Species alone may not be a meaningful criterion on which to draw moral lines, but there are
certainly moral lines to be drawn. The most significant
of these, perhaps, is between those animals that are or
are not sentient – which rather depends on how you
choose to define that word. Tom Regan initially applied
his theory of animal rights only to 'normal mammalians,

aged one or more', plus human babies, some birds, and possibly fish. Peter Singer wrote that his utilitarian considerations stretched to somewhere between the shrimp and the oyster, but did not include insects or spiders. Joan Dunayer, on the other hand – an author who advocates for animal rights – has stated that anything with a nervous system counts. Even houseflies should have equal rights, she has said, since each one 'is an individual who has a unique life experience and never will exist again.' Both Singer and Regan have found ways to show that the death of a human, all else being equal, is a more significant event than the death of an animal. Joan Dunayer disagrees.

Given that most proponents acknowledge that some distinctions between species must be made, yet disagree on what, where or why, anti-speciesism is a principle of limited usefulness. It sounds conclusive, but it's really just a gateway to more dispute. Importantly, I think, it is also a principle with a paradox trapped inside. The basic arguments of both utilitarians and animal rights proponents can be summarized like this:

Biologically, human beings are not different from animals in morally meaningful ways. Therefore, human beings should behave differently from animals in morally meaningful ways.

Anti-speciesists prove that animals are just like us in order to demonstrate why we should not behave like them.

That formula may seem facetious, but it opens the door to one of the strongest arguments against allowing animals the same moral consideration as humans. That is, that human morality is not a one-way street. It is, at least in theory, reciprocal. Treat others as you would have them treat you: *that* is the Golden Rule. We cannot extend that rule to animals, some would say, because we cannot expect that kind of reciprocity from them.

In making this point, however, one is immediately faced with the problem of what philosophers call 'marginal cases'. These are, if you like, the exceptions to the Golden Rule. Nobody expects moral reciprocity from babies, or from people with cognitive impairments, and yet, by and large, we extend our moral concern to them without question. So, why not animals? What exactly is the difference?

One answer to this would be to go a little further, and to deny outright the principle of anti-speciesism. Distinguishing by species is not morally indefensible, according to this view, it is perfectly reasonable. The philosopher Roger Scruton put it like this: 'It is in the nature of human beings that, in normal conditions, they become members of a moral community, governed by duty and protected by rights. Abnormality in this respect does not cancel membership.' To make such a claim is not to deny all moral consideration to animals, merely to deny them the same consideration as humans. Dogs and bears, writes Scruton, are simply *'not the kind of thing'* to which such consideration applies.

A second way to justify a moral distinction between

the 'marginal case' human and the animal is to acknowledge that it is illogical, but to deny that this is ethically
problematic. After all, such a distinction derives not
from logic but from sentiment, and most of us allow for
some partiality within our moral thinking. We allow for
someone to prefer the death of a stranger to that of a
friend or family member; we allow them to prefer the
death of a wild animal to that of a pet. Such attitudes are
clearly discriminatory, and run counter to the principle
of 'equal rights', but they are not immoral. Our concern
for babies over bears is perhaps the same kind of
distinction.

I find it easy to get caught up in arguments like these, to
be swayed back and forth by each challenge and each
response. There is persuasive logic at work on every side,
and the hammering and honing of ideas can be compelling. And yet, stepping back, it occurs to me that virtually
all of this debate takes place within a peculiar kind of bubble, from which vital context is entirely excluded. That
context is the world in which we – and animals – live.

The philosophy of animal rights has often been criticized
for failing to address wider questions about the environment, and indeed for actively opposing certain kinds of
environmental protection. By identifying sentience as
the sole criterion for inclusion in the realm of moral
concern, it leaves the majority of living things standing
outside that realm. A squirrel has rights and value,
according to this view, but an oak tree has neither. Nor
does a forest.

It's possible to argue that protecting the rights of sentient animals also means protecting the ecosystems on which they rely, but it's a deeply unsatisfying argument. Why should the value of a minnow be inherent, but the value of a river be conferred only by association? And why should an ecosystem that supports no sentient life – one that is rich only in plants, for instance – be considered to have no value whatsoever?

For me, this is one of the most glaring and consequential problems with the logic of animal rights, and with Peter Singer's utilitarianism. If the ability to feel pain is the only thing that matters, then most of the world is worthless. And even if you acknowledge that there may be other *kinds* of value, and other reasons not to do harm, to insist on the primacy of sentience as the basis for moral concern is to imagine the world in very peculiar ways. An ocean will always come second to a cod.

The origin of this problem is obvious. Though they may aspire to end human exploitation of our fellow creatures, these two theories are profoundly anthropocentric. Their starting point is the assumption that people have intrinsic moral worth. From there, they work outwards, conferring some of that moral worth, like magic dust, upon those animals that possess similar biological capabilities. They see value in those things that are most like humans, and are blind to it in those that are most different.

I think a coherent moral concern for the natural world should begin with a recognition, firstly, that lives have value whether they share a particular characteristic with humans or not, and secondly, that habitats and ecosystems have value independently of any animals – sentient or otherwise – that might rely on them. The question then becomes, *what* value, and how ought that value to be respected?

This is not an enquiry that can lead to simple answers, but even a crude attempt to consider it would surely need to start by acknowledging that every life, every *kind* of life, is different. A mountain gorilla is different from a field mouse is different from a stag beetle is different from a Scots pine is different from the Amazon rainforest. The way we think about these things, therefore, the way we value them or express our moral concern for them, should likewise be different. We can have empathic concern for creatures that experience pain and suffering, and rational concern for all living things, including ecosystems. We can have additional moral concern for human beings, with whom we share intricate social bonds and responsibilities.

The interests of individual animals, I would argue, cannot trump the interests of the biological communities of which they are a part. A healthy, functioning environment must be recognized as a good thing, in and of itself. It must be understood as more than just the sum of its sentient creatures. To me, these seem like self-evident truths, but for Tom Regan and other animal rights activists they are quite the opposite. To them, the rights of individuals are always, necessarily, the primary concern. To suggest otherwise, Regan has stated, is a serious moral failing.

This disagreement is instructive, for while the animal rights thinkers of the 1970s and 1980s usually aligned themselves with the progressive politics and civil rights movements of the 1960s, their absolute emphasis on individual interests can just as well be seen as a product of its own time, of the economic individualism at the forefront of British and American politics in that era. It is no surprise to me that the animal rights movement has been, in large part, a consumerist one, in which the kind of person you are is defined by what you buy. To be a good person, one merely has to stop consuming animal products, and perhaps encourage one's friends to do the same. Capitalism ensures that such a choice is easy; our supermarkets are well stocked for ethical convenience.

That convenience, I think, disguises the fact that things are never simple, and that no diet is harm-free. Forests are cut down to grow crops. Those crops are treated with chemicals that kill insects, molluscs and other creatures. When that crop is harvested, birds and mammals will be killed by the machinery. Wherever that crop is stored, rats and mice will be killed to keep it safe. When it is transported, greenhouse gases will be emitted. However it is packaged, waste will be produced. No one whose diet is dependent upon this reality should allow themselves to feel guiltless. There are many kinds of harm, and closing one's eyes to some of them is not morally righteous, it is just self-imposed ignorance. The world is not simple.

*

I learned to gut a fish when I was about twelve years old. I don't remember the details of the lesson, but I know that responsibility was the key reason behind it. If you are going to bring home fish, my mother insisted, you have to deal with the messy part too. In fact, compared to a mammal or a bird, gutting a fish is not a messy job at all. Two cuts are all that's required: one to remove the head, then a second slice from the anus up to the neck. Once the body is open, everything comes out in a slimy, sloppy handful.

Sometimes, out of curiosity, I will see what's left in the stomach, squeezing with my fingers or the flattened blade of my knife until the contents emerge. From that I can learn what the fish itself has been eating. Snails, caddis larvae, sticklebacks, midges. A mush of food within food. Occasionally, the guts will come out convulsing, with a cargo of parasitic worms that have temporarily outlived their host. The death for which I am responsible is only one in an endless muddle of killing and consumption.

These days, when I take a fish, I usually gut it straight away, holding it just above the water from which it came. The parts of the body for which I have no need are returned to that water. Something in there will have need of them; nothing will go to waste. What began as an act of convenience, of cleanliness, has become a way of giving back.

I am conscious, at such times, of how remote any strict moral theory seems from the reality of that fish, of those guts, of that water. How fragile and inadequate our ethical codes appear when considered in the places to which they are supposed to apply. Removed from the pages of a book, they float like cobwebs, held together by their own internal logic, but attached to the ground by nothing more solid than faith. In the forest or on a mountain, beside a river or at sea, they are lifted by the breeze and drift invisibly away.

More than any particular book or theory, I suspect, it is distance – literal, as well as figurative – from that muddle of life and death that is responsible for the idea that animals must be protected from harm. For most, that distance is just a matter of lifestyle, a separation from the natural world and from food production that now counts as normal. Not so long ago, people had complex, nuanced attitudes towards the creatures they ate. 'A peasant becomes fond of his pig and is glad to salt away its pork,' wrote John Berger. 'What is significant, and is so difficult for the urban stranger to understand, is that the two statements in that sentence are connected by an *and* and not by a *but*.' Today, few have the opportunity to know exactly what is meant by that conjunction. They close their eyes to the source of their food, or else they turn their noses up.

But there's something more than this, I think, something that hides behind the horror that many now feel towards meat. It is a moral flinch with deep, familiar roots. Implicit within animal rights thinking is the idea that evolution has bequeathed us a broken world, a flawed world, a morally repugnant world, in which creatures kill to live and suffer to be eaten. Human beings, according to this view, unique among animals, can rise above their wretchedness and help to minimize the suffering of the planet.

It does not take a theologian to spot the similarities between this way of thinking and Christianity, or to see how the notion of animal rights is connected to that of souls and sanctity. The whole concept of 'inherent value' takes its resonance directly from religion. Behind both, of course, is the age-old fear of death, the ultimate motivating force. And that fear – of our own part in the endless recycling of energy on which all life relies – can easily turn towards biophobia, a hatred of life as it actually exists.

In a much-discussed article in the *New York Times* from 2010, the philosopher Jeff McMahan wrote that he was 'inclined to embrace the heretical conclusion that we have reason to desire the extinction of all carnivorous species'. And he meant it, too. Though the implications of his view were principally theoretical, McMahan explicitly argued that allowing endangered predators such as the Siberian tiger to go extinct may be the ethical thing to do.

I suspect that most moderate supporters of animal rights would rear back from this idea. They would argue that their judgements only apply to human actions (that weird paradox of anti-speciesism again). But McMahan's views cannot be disowned so easily. After all, if an animal's rights are truly inherent, if the harm it suffers is as worthy of consideration as that of any human, then surely the desire to end all predation is not an 'heretical conclusion' at all. It is pure, perfect logic.

It is also preposterous.

The harm suffered by animals in the course of their lives – including being killed and eaten by other animals – is not a moral problem. It is life itself. It is how the whole thing works. 'There is no death that is not somebody's food,' wrote the poet Gary Snyder, and 'no life that is not somebody's death'. To imagine that human beings can, like the angels, rise above all this and wash their hands of harm, is fantasy. It is a moral hubris that is entirely detached from those lives about which its proponents claim to care.

Many indigenous cultures are far more adept at dealing with the facts of life than we, today, in the West. They understand that death is an irresolvable issue. The interests of all living things cannot be compatible with each other, for life requires the opposite. Part of what living things *are* is food for other living things. This goes for sentient creatures as much as it does for plants. Each death is both bad and good, each one both an ending and a beginning. Some cultures have dealt with this paradox through rituals of propitiation, of giving thanks to the animal or plant that is eaten, or to the place from which it has come. According to Robin Wall Kimmerer, an American biologist and a member of the Citizen Potawatomi Nation, such ceremonies 'have the power to focus attention to a way of living awake in the world'.

To see value only in the span of each creature's existence, bookended by birth and death, is to miss a great deal. It is to miss the extraordinary magic of the whole process of living, the birth and death and rebirth that goes on all around and within us, over which we have no power and from which we cannot escape. An engagement with this process, I think, inclines us towards humility, and towards gratitude. I experience that humility and that gratitude most often when I am fishing.

To my mind, the philosophies of animal rights and animal liberation both fail in their efforts to codify human behaviour towards other creatures. They fail, principally, because neither theory attempts to engage with the world as it really is. Both are profoundly anthropocentric, and both seek to brush aside the complexities of biology, to impose straight lines where none can be drawn. Neither of these theories articulates any kind of love for or intimacy with the natural world. Instead, they seem motivated by a deep revulsion at that world, and their prescription – that we should withdraw even further from nature – only emphasizes this biophobia. I don't find that prescription persuasive or desirable.

This is not to say, of course, that seeking to reduce the harm we inflict as individuals is a poor moral choice. Nor is it to say that the judgements of animal rights thinkers are always wrong. To feel disgusted by factory farming is understandable, for instance, because factory farming *is* disgusting. There are good environmental reasons to condemn it, and there are good ethical reasons to condemn it. But I do not believe there are good ethical reasons for us never to eat animals. And I do not believe there are good ethical reasons for us not to catch fish with a rod and line.

The condemnation of angling, and of eating meat in

general, is different from the condemnation of factory farming. Disgust at the latter cannot be reasonably extended to encompass the former. It is another kind of disgust altogether. Opposition to angling is born out of an increasing disconnection from nature, a disconnection that has led, quite understandably, to a kind of loathing for the basic facts of human and animal life. It is born from a desire to escape from the moral muddle upon which these facts insist. It is born from our fear of death, and our wish to be rid of reminders that we are mortal. And it is born from an economy that allows us to eat whatever we please while closing our eyes to how that food is produced.

Many anglers (like many hunters, I'm told) experience a pang of remorse when they kill a fish – though remorse is not quite the right word. Some describe it as guilt or regret, but these terms don't feel adequate either. This feeling, whatever one calls it, is an emotional connection to the natural world, and a recognition of the irresolvable tensions that exist in that world, from which we humans, try as we might, cannot escape.

Too often a fear of doubt induces us to ignore the competing instincts within ourselves, and to build a comfortable cloak of false conviction. Killing is a significant and complicated act, and the feelings that arise from that act are, I think, important. They are part of what makes us human, and part of what makes us animal. 'I have thought a great deal about carnivorousness,' wrote the American author Annie Dillard. 'I eat meat. These things are not issues; they are mysteries.'

To be seduced by the promise of moral certainty is to fail fully to engage with the world in which we live. That world is messy, and to imagine otherwise is a failure to see or to think clearly. An ethical person is not one who believes they have the answers, but one who continues to ask the questions. Angling, for me, has become part of that questioning, whether I kill a fish or not. It is an active engagement with moral ambiguity, a *leaning towards* rather than a *flinching away*. It is a reminder, always, that my presence affects others, that I am complicit in the living and the dying of the world, and that I could not relinquish that complicity, even if I wanted to.

THE
RIVER CLYDE

South Lanarkshire, 2020

IT WAS EARLY NOVEMBER, AND I was up to my knees in the River Clyde, casting within the shadow of a concrete bridge. Or I would have been within its shadow, had there been enough light to create one. But on that morning, light was a limited resource. The icy clarity I'd hoped for when I left the house had not materialized. Instead, the world was muted and murky, as though someone had thrown a hessian sack over the sun.

I flicked the pair of heavy nymphs upstream, towards the brisk central current. I let them drift within it, keeping the rod tip high, watching the line for signs of life, then drew them up and out again, with a single movement of my wrist: a steady lift that ended with a sideways swipe. The flies returned to the water with a plop.

The Clyde is not a name that widely conjures thoughts of aquatic riches. Like other waterways that flow through industrial cities, this river developed a reputation for filthiness. And while that reputation was at one time well deserved, it no longer tells the whole story. Even in Glasgow, as the river nears the sea and takes on a brown, soupy appearance, the water is cleaner than it has been in a very long time. Hundreds of millions of pounds have been spent reducing pollution and making the river more hospitable for fish and for other life. Salmon have returned, both to the Clyde and its tributaries, and the river is home to many large trout.

The Clyde is also beautiful, particularly in its highest reaches. If you've ever taken the train between London and Glasgow, you've probably seen it. The West Coast Main Line passes close to the source, and follows it downstream for miles. Many who gaze out on that glittering slice of silver would never guess that it's the same river that later roils darkly through the city. Those highest reaches were where I was that morning, within sight of the train line and within earshot of the M74 motorway. All around were fields of sheep and cattle, their pasture fading from bright autumn greens towards the drab hues of winter.

The reason I was there that day, in November of all months, was neither trout nor salmon (the season for both of which was then closed) but grayling: another species for which this river is home. I have a fondness for grayling that is, I must admit, based more on aesthetics than it is on familiarity. I find them exceedingly pretty fish, shimmering silver-grey like brushed steel. Visibly salmonids – distant cousins of trout, char and salmon – they nevertheless have a number of distinguishing features. Their scales, for one thing, tend to be more pronounced than those of their relatives, and their mouths, for another, tend to be smaller, with a more prominent 'nose' out front. They're more snouty than trouty, you might say. Most distinctive of all, though, the feature for which they are best known, is their dorsal fin, a broad banner of a thing, a sail fit for the high seas. Extended, the fin looks out of proportion to the fish, like a man with hands the size of doormats. They've struck me always as special fish, delicately beautiful but with more than a hint of swagger.

Despite this fondness, though, I haven't actually seen that many of them. Not face to face, as it were. The first I ever caught were in Alaska, at a place called, aptly, Grayling Lake. Those were of a different species to the ones that live in Britain – *Thymallus arcticus* rather than *Thymallus thymallus* – but visually, the two are very similar. I caught a pair of them that day, despite being so terrified of bears that I wasn't able to enjoy the fishing at all. I killed the larger of the two fish and ate it that night, fried in butter. If the flesh did indeed carry the smell or flavour of thyme, as its Latin name insists, it was too subtle for my palate to pick out. Instead, it had the sweet, satisfying taste of danger.

Since then, my encounters with grayling have been infrequent (and thankfully less fraught with dread than the first). Each one I catch feels novel, and carries with it the excitement of the unfamiliar.

I have two excuses for the rarity of these catches. First, grayling thrive in just a handful of Scottish rivers, in only one of which I have ever cast a line. Second, they are most often fished for in winter, after the brown trout season has ended. They tend to shoal in the coldest months, so catches can be best when the weather is at its worst. On the chilliest of days, though, I struggle to summon the necessary enthusiasm for standing crotch-deep in freezing rivers. I ought to claim otherwise, I know. I ought to boast of my willingness to suffer for this art. But that would be a lie. When the temperature drops below a certain level, my eagerness likewise declines. I look out of the window, then I look at the sofa, the radiator, the kettle. Most often, home comforts win. But not every time. Not that day.

Grayling aren't native to this river – nor, in fact, to any of the rivers in Scotland in which they now live. They were brought to the Clyde by members of a local angling club, in 1855, arriving by steam train at a now-defunct station not far from where I was standing. I like to think of them on that train, puff-puffing its way north, across the border, bringing them to their new home. There were three dozen in that first shipment, and many more were brought two years later. The introduction proved a great success, and was followed by further introductions, both official and unofficial, elsewhere in the country.

Probably because these fish didn't come far – just a couple of hundred miles, from Derbyshire – the ecosystem here adapted easily to their presence. There were some grumbles early on that the average size of trout declined after the arrival of grayling, but there's no evidence that this was truly the case. As a general rule, moving species around like this often has unintended negative consequences, knocking ecosystems out of balance; but in the case of grayling, it's almost as though they were here all along.

The same cannot be said, however, for signal crayfish, an American species with which the Clyde seems, in some places, to be infested. Beneath the bridge where I was standing, dozens of these creatures were gathered, like a congregation of little boiled lobsters around my feet. There was something alarming, almost loathsome about them, a feeling compounded by knowledge of the harm they do. Introduced to the UK in the 1970s to be farmed as food, these intrepid crustaceans quickly escaped and spread, creating an ecological mess as they went. Each individual of this species carries a fungal disease that is fatal to the native white-clawed crayfish, which now, predictably, is endangered. Furthermore, the signal crayfish – which are larger and more aggressive than the native species – eat fish eggs, amphibians and insects in enormous numbers, and indeed have a significant detrimental impact on the invertebrate life of rivers. Once established, they are impossible to get rid of. Though unwelcome, they're going nowhere.

I wound in my line, stepped carefully around the

horde of brandished claws, then headed downstream, pausing only once or twice along the way. I followed the meanders of the river, past sluggish pools and shallow runs for three-quarters of a mile or so, then turned around and began to fish back up again. Unhurriedly, attentively, I cast.

There is plenty of good water in this part of the river. By which I mean the kind of water that induces optimism; the kind of water that looks like the kind of water that, if I were a fish, I would choose to inhabit. Which is not to say that my own tastes and the fishes' are always aligned. They're not. But it doesn't matter too much. So long as the water looks good, the optimism comes easy. Find one grayling, I figured, and I would likely find more. I only needed to get it right once.

I made it as far as lunchtime without getting it right, without even so much as a hint that fish were present. And by that time, I'd covered a *lot* of good water. I was more than halfway back to the bridge, at a deep, straight-sided pool, slow at the tail end, boisterous at the head. The pool looked hopeful, like the right kind of place, and I stopped to eat before giving it a go. I sat high on the bank in my waders and laid my shoulder bag down beside me. It was soaked through – I'd gone in too deep, several times – but my food, ensconced in plastic, was still dry. I pulled a pack of oatcakes out, and several thick wedges of cheddar. I leaned back on the bank and chewed happily.

Eager as I nearly always am to keep fishing, I still very

often find that lunch can be a highlight of a day out. Something about the state of mind that angling induces makes for a quite different experience than an ordinary picnic. Senses are attuned. Eyes and ears are at their keenest. Even tastebuds can seem primed for optimal performance, turning cheap cheese into pure luxury.

Often, while I'm doing this, while I'm eating, as close to silent as my jaws will allow, I'll imagine the water in front of me to be transparent. Truly transparent. I'll imagine I can see right through it, as if it were a bowl, and that every fish in the place is visible. I'll scan back and forth, looking at each trout, each grayling in turn, seeing where it lies and how it holds in the current, until something – the *grawk* of a passing raven, the barking of a dog, or in this case the rattle of a northbound train – brings me back to the unimagined. Once again, the dim light reflecting off the pool's surface hides everything within.

I picked up the rod and stepped back into the water, fished my way up towards the upper end, where the current galloped in. It was deep there, and the flow was fast enough to make fishing awkward, dragging my flies away before they ever reached the bottom. I changed to the heaviest nymphs I had and tried again. Once, twice. The line paused oddly and I lifted the rod tip, felt a liveliness that drew back against me, a conviction without real strength. I stripped the line in to find what I'd been looking for, or near enough: an eight-inch grayling that came swiftly to my hand, fluttering as it reached the surface, like a light blinking in the fog. I knelt down to unhook it, and it took the opportunity to escape, shaking the fly from its mouth just as my fingers went around it. I watched the space where it had been for a second longer, as if it might somehow reappear in my hand and allow me a closer look. But the fish had vanished, leaving only relief, and the eagerness to catch another.

As I stood again, I turned to my right and was taken aback to see an older man, also fishing, just ten metres away, at the very top of the pool. He was the first person I'd seen since I arrived, and the sound of the river had concealed his approach. At the very moment I looked up, the man's rod bent over, and he proceeded to haul in a grayling of his own, considerably larger than the one I'd just caught. He brought it to the bank then let it go, and took a few more steps towards me.

The most basic rule of angling etiquette states that you keep your distance from other people, you give them space, and you don't step into water they're about to fish. Which is exactly what the man had done to me. But the problem with rules of etiquette is that, when someone else ignores them, there's not much you can do in response without resorting to pettiness of your own. It was clear there were fish in this pool, and if I stayed I would likely catch more. But the man had no intentions of making way, so staying could mean a confrontation. And since there is nothing I like less than confrontation, I shook my head and gave in. I wound my line as loudly as I could manage – which isn't very loud – then went over to speak, as though everything were fine.

'Any luck?' I asked, not letting on that I had seen him land a fish.

'Just one,' he said.

'Any size?'

He shrugged. 'It was just a grayling.'

I suppose I could have pointed out that, if he were trying to catch anything other than grayling, in November, in this river, he was breaking more than just rules of etiquette. He was breaking the law. But if that's what he was doing then he probably didn't need me to tell him, and it probably wouldn't have gone down well if I'd tried. So instead, I just nodded and turned away, then walked upstream until I was out of sight, grumbling silently to myself as I went.

The irritation I felt was not just about the man's manners, if I'm honest. It was also about the man himself. Though there are a handful of people whose company I will eagerly seek when fishing, and though many of the happiest times I've spent by the water have been in that company, for the most part these days I am a solitary angler. Perhaps it's all the years I spent in Shetland, where even sharing a loch is almost never necessary, but some days – and this, certainly, was one – I take other people's presence as a personal affront. It is a selfish, irrational and unshakeable feeling. I don't go fishing in search of 'peace and quiet', exactly; I get plenty of that at home. But when I fish, I want to choose the company I keep, or else choose to keep none at all. Sometimes other people – anglers, swimmers, jet-skiers – can feel like an invasion of a privacy that, in this public space, is only ever a kind of fantasy.

There were a few more pools to try on the way back to the car, and I paused to cast, here and there, but with little real enthusiasm. Having abandoned the one spot where I'd found fish, my confidence had not come with me. I'd left it beneath the man's boots, along with most of the cheer I'd mustered through the day. But I kept on, casting and walking, casting and walking, until I was back, just downstream of the bridge where I'd begun. Distracted, I tried to make the best of this last chance, covering all of the water I was able to reach, moving a step or two between each cast, my eyes and thoughts wandering, my annoyance unappeased.

As I came back under the shadow of the bridge again, I was conscious, suddenly, of a swift-moving shape to my left, a hurtling at the edge of my vision, and then a splash as that shape hit the water. There seemed to be a brief commotion, as if whatever it was that had fallen was thrashing in the current. And then it stopped.

From where I was standing, I couldn't tell at all what I had seen, or what I was looking at, but I kept looking, waiting for it to be carried towards me. I stood on my tiptoes, turned my head, trying to shift the shape into clarity. I watched it float downstream, saw it sharpen into a ruffled blob of black and white, and then, eventually, a bird. A male goosander. Entirely dead.

In such moments, the mind goes hunting for an explanation, for a good reason why what has happened has just happened. It tries to conjure the unknown from the known. But I couldn't find a reason – not one that would convince me. Had someone thrown a dead goosander from a moving car as they drove past? That would account for everything I'd seen, but it hardly seemed plausible.

Perhaps, instead, in its final, dying moments, the bird had rested on the bridge until it toppled and flapped its last. That was more likely, certainly, though I still was not quite persuaded.

I wound my line in for the last time and bit off the flies, then hooked them to the drying patch on the back of my bag. Perhaps, I thought, the bird had just had enough, had given up on life, on its litany of petty frustrations, and had dropped from the sky in mortal despair.

I watched, unenlightened, as the dead goosander drifted downstream, making its way, effortlessly, towards the bright lights and bustle of Glasgow.

THE POSSIBILITY
OF MONSTERS

THE ENORMOUS VARIATION THAT EXISTS between and within fish species is the biological quirk on which the entire sport of angling rests. And the most significant of these variable traits is size. An Atlantic blue marlin is bigger than a wels catfish, which is bigger than a small-mouth bass, which is bigger than a common dace. From finger-length to many times the weight of a human being, fish come in all sizes. But it is the variability *within* species that makes angling most interesting. If it weren't for that, this would all be just a numbers game.

An adult brown trout in overcrowded or nutrient-poor water might be six inches long. But in ideal conditions, that fish could grow a great deal larger. In a lake or river with a healthy breeding population, there should be individuals in a broad range of sizes, such that you cannot know how big the next fish you catch will be. This is where much of the joy and anticipation of angling lies: the uncertainty, the possibility, the wondering.

Most anglers begin small. Every fish is exciting when you're young, and those that are most visible, most catchable, are often most exciting of all. The tiddlers that shoal in the shallows are an enticement to children. They are proof that magical things live below the surface. I spent an inordinate amount of time as a youngster catching little roach, baby coalfish, tiny trout. They were all I needed to make a day by the water worthwhile. To bring one of those little lives to my hand was the greatest thrill I could imagine.

But it doesn't take long, usually, before bigger fish loom into view. A colossal splash by the lily pads, an arm-length shadow, glimpsed and then gone: the evidence for more substantial things will be seen by anyone who pays attention to water.

The first big fish I ever saw were carp, in milky brown Sussex lakes. I was eleven or twelve then, fishing during summer holidays, while visiting my father. I would skewer maggots or sweetcorn on to a hook, then sit on a folding chair and wait for my float to duck and disappear. The fish I caught were mostly roach and rudd and perch, and they were rarely much longer than my hand. But in some of those lakes there were common and mirror carp, which would loll around on the surface, fat, slow and lazy. They always seemed to be a little beyond my casting distance, and a long way beyond my ability to catch them. But every now and then, someone else on the lake would hook one, and I would drop my rod and run to get a closer look. They were not enormous for their kind, those fish – ten pounds, fifteen pounds, sometimes twenty – but to me, they were as big as my greatest ambitions.

I learned to catch them in the end, after several summers of trying. Not the largest ones, which always eluded me, but their younger, more reckless cousins – fish that made the perch and rudd look like minnows. Six pounds, at a guess, was my best one, caught on a floating dog biscuit when I was fourteen years old. It was a little carp, really, but it was big to me.

There were other fish as well, around that same time, and in various places. There were Pacific salmon – sockeye and humpback – caught during a holiday to Vancouver Island. They came for lurid rubber squid dragged deep behind a motorboat in the ocean, which felt a long way from the kind of fishing I was used to. Then, when I was sixteen, there was a tench of almost seven pounds, soft-bellied and slimy, caught on a baking hot day when there was no one with me to witness it.

For the most part, though, big fish were beyond reach for me back then. In Shetland, where I lived and did most of my fishing, what I caught were generally on the smaller side of average. A trout above half a pound was a good one, as far as I was concerned. Double that was a rarity. Yet every time I went to the clubhouse of the Shetland Anglers Association – which I did most weeks from my early teens, to the bemusement, and perhaps irritation, of the senior members, who went to chat, drink and throw darts in peace – I was faced with the physical embodiment of what I wasn't catching. The casts of two brown trout hung on the wall: one dark, red-spotted fish that had weighed over six pounds, and another, much paler, that had been more than nine.

I used to look at those two trout with something like awe, hardly able to believe they had once swum. And in waters so close by. I was fascinated then, as most young anglers are, by the possibility of monsters, by the fish so far beyond the norm that they stretch the imagination, and expand the limits of what one can wish for.

At some point in my youth, an acquaintance of my mother's passed on a stack of old copies of *Angling Times* and *Angler's Mail*, and I read that pile of pages compulsively. I cut out pictures of flabby carp, and the grinning men who were holding them. I stuck the pictures on my wall, the way other boys I knew were sticking up pictures of footballers. I had no interest in kicking a ball around, or in watching other people kick. Not then, not now. I just wanted to catch big fish.

Yet, despite this intense desire, I recognized even then that size is a funny thing in fishing. I knew perfectly well that a six-pound carp was nothing to boast about, but a six-pound wild brown trout could be stuffed and mounted for public display. I knew, as well, that a big trout in Shetland was smaller than a big trout in New Zealand, and that each piece of water I visited would have its own unique scale, from little to large. All of it, I understood, was relative, and any dream of big fish had to be elastic.

Not everyone is content with relativity, however. For some, only the absolute is worth pursuing.

Improvements in the strength of fishing tackle over the years have vastly expanded the list of what can be caught and where. In past centuries, lines were woven from silk or horse hair, and the inherent fragility of those materials meant that much of the underwater world remained unreachable. Put too much strain on and the line would snap. The same was true of rods. The limits of what they could do were easily exceeded.

By the early twentieth century, however, anglers were beginning to figure out how to catch some of the biggest fish in the sea. Marlin, sailfish, tuna, sharks: a host of colossal species could be found across the world's oceans, and could in theory be targeted by recreational fishermen. In order to successfully hook and reel them in, though, anglers faced three major challenges: technological, physiological and piscine.

The technological challenges were obvious. To catch fish that could reach hundreds, sometimes thousands of pounds in weight, the tackle had to be able to cope. The rod couldn't break under the pressure. The line would have to be immensely strong. Reels would have to hold a huge quantity of that line, and be able to let it out at high speed, without overheating or falling apart.

The physiological challenges were equally clear. How

does a human being haul in a fish that is many times larger than themselves? How could anyone *control* such a fish? Extreme strength was required, and endurance too. An angler might spend many hours attached to a fish before it was exhausted enough to be dragged to the boat. Keeping that angler hydrated and preventing them from being pulled overboard were essential.

The piscine challenges were less predictable, but ultimately proved the most difficult to overcome. Once hooked, any fish, no matter how large, can become a target for aquatic predators. Thrashing about, unable to swim as it wishes, it will quickly draw attention to itself. And since sharks are often numerous in the same places in which other big fish live, that attention could be a real problem. As they were pulled towards the boat, marlin and tuna would invariably be attacked, eaten alive, so that by the time they were brought on board, little more than a head, and sometimes a tail and backbone, would remain. These grotesque, mutilated trophies would be brought to shore and strung up beside the angler for a photograph. Such pictures were supposed to convey the enormity of the catch, the sheer awesomeness of these fish. But they conveyed other things too.

The first person known to have landed a large Atlantic bluefin tuna intact was Ernest Hemingway. He caught it in May of 1935, off the Bahamas, then proceeded to catch many more. Hemingway was a dedicated 'big game' angler, and spent much of his time fishing, mostly around Cuba, where he lived on and off for more than two decades. He was fascinated by the fish he sought, and

conducted research on their habits, distribution and dif-
ferentiation. He worked hard to overcome the various
challenges that catching these species entailed; and to a
great extent, he succeeded.

Hemingway's initial method for deterring shark
attacks was to shoot at them with a Thompson subma-
chine gun. He soon discovered, though, that this brutal
technique only made matters worse, since it increased
the quantity of blood in the water, and so attracted yet
more sharks. His next idea was more sensible, but equally
telling.

Because sharks would attack when a hooked fish was
worn out, Hemingway's solution was to never let them
tire completely. To hang on until a fish is exhausted, he
came to believe, to let your tackle do all the work, was
unsporting. Instead, you had to fight. You had to pull
with every ounce of strength your body could muster,
and then keep pulling. 'For half an hour, an hour, or five
hours,' he wrote, before abandoning all punctuation in
his excitement, 'you are fastened to the fish as much as
he is fastened to you and you tame him and break him
the way a wild horse is broken and finally lead him to the
boat.' Getting the fish on board, though, was pretty much
beside the point; 'it is while you are fighting him that is
the fun.'

For Hemingway, the *physical* challenge was the main
attraction, the source of the pleasure in this pursuit. And
I suspect this attitude is shared by many big-game
anglers. After all, this kind of fishing doesn't require a
great deal of skill. You just drag your baits or lures around

and wait for something to bite. It's a pretty basic business, all things considered, and hooking a fish is mostly a matter of luck. What counts, then, is not the hooking or the landing or the surroundings or the meditative nature of the activity, or anything else that anglers often point to as reasons for their strange behaviour. It is the long, arduous battle between macho man and fish.

Macho man . . . or woman.

In an essay about catching marlin, titled 'The Young Woman and the Sea', Ernest Hemingway's granddaughter, Lorian, insisted that 'Papa' had been right all along. 'There is not another strength as holy and unrestrained as the strength of that one beautifully mad fish,' she wrote. 'Before, I had thought it was all foolishness, this man's business of fighting a fish. But it is not.'

Later, though, in an addendum to that essay, Lorian Hemingway recanted. She condemned the 'wholesale slaughter' that then was common to this kind of angling, especially in the tournaments in which she – and her grandfather before her – had taken part. 'I cannot participate,' she explained, 'in the slow and certain decimation of these fish populations.' From then on, her fishing was confined to lakes and streams.

Since those words were written, there has been a move towards catch-and-release methods by anglers seeking big-game species. In response to declining populations, some countries now insist that all marlin are returned to the water alive – which is not a big ask, given that the fight is the point. By the time it gets to the boat, the fish has done its job. It has been cast as the great adversary in a mock battle between David and Goliath (albeit a battle in which the scales are tipped, by technology, in favour of David). The fish is a prop, as it was in those gruesome photographs taken at the dockside: man with mutilated marlin. It is sought and caught in order for the man to prove his manliness, to demonstrate – to himself, as much as anyone else, I think – his strength and stamina.

Nobody who catches a six-pound trout, or even a thirty-pound carp, could persuade themselves that their physical strength is being tested to the limit. A good fish will take some persuading to come shoreward on light tackle, and if you're unlucky it might even leave you with an aching wrist, but a trout or a carp is not going to pull you in the water and drag you away. It's just not that kind of fight.

So if one's brawn is not in question, if shoring up one's machismo is not the point, then what is the appeal of a largeness that is only relative? To put it another way, what exactly is the appeal of big small fish?

I think most anglers, if asked, would point to the difficulty of catching them, to the challenge and the sense of achievement that is felt when you do. And they wouldn't be wrong. Catching a big trout is generally more difficult than catching a small one, and not just because there are fewer of them. Big fish have a reputation for being wary or even 'smart', and it may be true that they develop a more acute sense of caution as they get older. Or, just as likely, those that are most attuned to the possible dangers they face are those that will survive the longest.

But increased size also allows fish to minimize their risk-taking. The biggest fish in a river can hog the best spot, with the most reliable food source. It can barge all challengers out of the way. Once there, it can afford to play it safe. All the food it wants will arrive in front of its nose. The smaller fish, in less productive locations, will have a harder time. They may need to take chances in order to fill their bellies. That odd-looking insect drifting by? That might be worth a bite.

To catch the larger, well-fed fish, then, the angler needs it to make a mistake. In order to do that, they must avoid making mistakes of their own. Casts should land in the right place, and delicately enough that they will not attract suspicion. The angler should avoid being seen or heard by the fish. They should avoid casting shadows on the water. The depth at which that fish is feeding may well matter; is it taking insects from the surface or the bottom, or from somewhere in between? Sometimes, the fly itself might be important: the size, the shape, the way it moves.

A certain degree of skill is usually required to hook a bigger fish, then, though luck and conditions will also play their part. Skill is needed, too, to bring it to the net, because that fish, once hooked, will do its damndest to get away. The feelings that come, therefore, when the fish has been landed and all uncertainty is over, are these: relief, exhilaration, the fizzing afterglow of nervous tension, admiration for the fish, and yes, some admiration for one's own achievement, some smugness at getting things right.

One might suspect that bragging rights are part of the appeal as well, and for some people that must be true. Those grinning anglers with the pot-bellied carp, whose photographs I gathered in my teens, may gain some pleasure at the thought of others' envy. (I'm told, too, that dating apps, particularly in the United States, are full of men whose profile pictures show them holding enormous fish – a frankly baffling phenomenon.) But the big fish seekers I know are not like that at all. Most of them are content to keep their best fish to themselves. That way, they won't get asked where they caught them. When they take photographs, it is not for other people's benefit, but for their own, in order to hold on to that fish and that moment in the only way they can.

It's been said that anglers start out by trying to catch the *most* fish, then move on to the *biggest* fish, and finally graduate to chasing the most *difficult* fish. But I don't subscribe to this view. For me, fishing just isn't like that. It's not a video game, at which one progresses, level after level, towards the top. There is nothing, in the end, to be achieved. I'm reminded here of the Scottish writer and hillwalker Nan Shepherd, who counselled against the peak-bagging tendencies of mountaineers. One can find a richer experience by learning to go *into* the hills, as she put it, not just *up* them.

There are anglers I follow on social media whose sole quarry are stunted brook trout in the streams of

Appalachia. A few inches long at most, those fish are like tiny sunsets: dark greens, golds and luminous orange, condensed into a thing that swims. There are anglers in Japan who compete to catch the smallest fish they possibly can, using the lightest of rods and lines and the tiniest hooks imaginable. There are anglers who just want an easy life, and see no appeal whatsoever in difficulty. In fact, the great freedom that this absurdity brings – the inherent absurdity of relative size – is that, if you want to, you can shrug it all off. You can enjoy yourself and challenge yourself in whatever way most appeals. Every day's fishing can be different. Some days I want numbers; I want to catch as many as I can, no matter the size. Other times I'm happy to hardly fish at all, but just to sit on the bank and let the day pass by. Mostly, I'm pleased with whatever comes my way.

My brother Rory, however, likes chasing big fish. More accurately, I could say that he likes *catching* big fish, but since the catching of them involves, in my experience, an inordinate amount of chasing, I have to assume that he enjoys that part of it too. What he's after are specimen trout, well above the average size – which in Shetland, where he still lives, is less than a pound. He's looking for fish that are out of the ordinary.

Me, I like ordinary. Ordinary suits me fine. I like the variety that comes with ordinary angling, the never knowing what you might catch next. To chase only monsters seems to me to be missing half the fun. It seems an awful lot like work. But he's my brother, so what can I do? Occasionally I have to join him.

On a late July afternoon, during one of my recent visits to Shetland, Rory and I were discussing our options, deciding where we ought to go the following evening. He mentioned a place I hadn't thought of in years. It was a loch he'd heard rumours about, up on a hill, not easily accessible from the road. He knew someone who knew someone, he said, who thought the fish there were enormous.

I know well that kind of rumour chain, and I know it can mean many things. The information might be years old, and any fish long dead. The information might be only conjecture, in which case Rory was just an eager guinea pig, testing a lazy angler's hunch. The information might also be plain wrong.

My curiosity was piqued, though, because I knew this loch. I had been there once already, years before. I had gone on that occasion to stock it, pouring bags of trout fry in, with three other local anglers. Back then, it was believed to have no fish at all, and the Shetland Anglers Association had a programme of stocking lochs like that, in the hope that a population could be restored. It was one of only a few such trips I ever took part in, so I remember it clearly, and I remember thinking that one day I would go back. But I never did. As far as I heard, no one ever caught one of those trout we put in. For whatever reason, they just disappeared. It happens.

But that was fifteen years ago. Maybe even twenty. Was it possible some of those fish could have survived that long? I checked online, but the information was contradictory. Brown trout have a life expectancy of five years, one website said. Another claimed they could live up to eighteen, or even more. Every source I checked gave a different figure, and I struggled to determine which was most reliable. If I believed those bigger numbers, then maybe, just maybe, a few of the fish we stocked could still be alive. And if they were, how big would they be? My imagination ran wild.

We'll try there, I said.

We parked up beside a broad metal gate, on a quiet road, just after seven the following evening. The air was cool for July, though not for Shetland, but the breeze was light. Thin clouds were threatening to disperse. We crossed the gate, then set off towards the south, over bog and tall heather. As the ground steepened, we had to lift our legs high to keep moving, and I felt myself winded by the effort. I paused to get my breath back, then continued, raising my knees and striding, making slow progress up the hill.

It took twenty minutes or so to get up and over the ridge, to where we could see the loch. Two *bonxies* – great skuas, wide-winged and fierce – were patrolling this higher ground, and they swooped close to assess the danger. A few weeks earlier in the breeding season and they would have been less accommodating, dive-bombing us as we approached. But they seemed content on this occasion to let us pass.

The loch itself was bigger than I remembered, perhaps ten acres in size, where in my mind it had been half that, or even smaller. The breeze was from the east, making both of the loch's longer banks fishable, so we picked one side each and separated.

I walked down to where a fence ended, several feet out in the water. I am always drawn to start at points like this, arbitrary landmarks, or watermarks, as it were. I don't know what it is about such features – fences, narrow bays, rocky outcrops, promontories – but in their disruption of a shore they seem to offer a way in, and give a hopeful sense of shape to a day.

I watched Rory walk carefully around the western end of the loch, then crouch down and start casting from behind a crop of soft rush on the bank. The plant was everywhere here, and keeping flies away from it was critical. The thick tussocks are like magnets for hooks, and even a glancing touch is enough for the stems to grab hold of your line and not let go. Remaining inconspicuous meant keeping casts high, and I saw Rory's arm raised well above his head, with only the slightest disturbance as his fly line hit the water.

It can be hard to know how to begin in a place like this, what tactics have the best hope of success. Bigger trout in Shetland are often caught on lures and streamers, imitations of small fish, on which those trout might be feeding. But given the lack of breeding opportunities here, I suspected that there were no small fish in this loch, and so perhaps what bigger ones there were would not be fooled that way. Instead, I tied on a couple of sizeable nymphs, one of them with a bit of weight to pull it down, and started casting.

The water, as one would expect in a location like this,

was peaty, somewhat murky, hardly ideal conditions for large fish or the rich insect life they would need to survive. I already had some doubts about the rumours Rory had heard, and they were not dispelled by initial impressions. Fishing is fuelled by hopeful tension and the ever-present possibility of success. Not being sure if there are, in fact, any fish at all in a loch, doesn't help to sustain such expectations. I cast carefully for a time, looking for signs of trout, but I felt myself relaxing. I felt my attention wane.

I changed flies after a while and moved a little farther down the bank. I put on a floating sedge pattern, with a sunk nymph behind it, cast out, left it for a moment, then slowly, splashily retrieved. I'd seen nothing rising so far, and there were few insects in the air, but sometimes fish will come up anyway, if you catch their attention and make the effort seem worthwhile.

Nothing came up. My attention drifted again. My eyes lifted from the line.

There were two families of red-throated divers on this loch. The surface, and sometimes the sky above, were busy with their presence. Every so often, one group would come too close to another, and a disagreement would ensue. Some of them would take flight, circle around the hill a few times, then splash back down into the water. The lowering light was punctured by the mournful, shimmering wails of those birds.

Then, not quite in the centre of my vision, but off to one side, close to shore, twenty metres or so down the bank from where I stood, a rise. A subtle disturbance on the surface, just the tiniest of dimples. I crept forward quickly, halving the distance between me and the fish, and cast my flies, once, then again. And again. Nothing happened. I waited, in case it reappeared, but everything was still. I cast again. A little closer, a little farther. Nothing.

But things had changed after that. A question had been answered. It was impossible to tell what size that fish might have been. But it *was* a fish, and that made all the difference.

And then there was another.

Farther down the bank, towards the northeast corner, a bigger rise, much splashier this time – a half-jump, you might call it. I weighed the options: stick with this fish, which had so far shown no interest, or try the other one? I waited to see if that second trout would show itself again. It did. Another rise, more subtle this time, but still clearly visible from forty yards away. I started walking, kept myself as low to the ground as I could without falling over. I slowed as I got close, stepped quietly, then started to cast.

It was getting on for 10 p.m., and the light was yellowing, with a little time still to go before the sun set. I covered all of the water in front of me, drawing the sedge in tiny jerks towards the shore, one cast then another. I tried again, laid the line out to my left, let it sit ten seconds, then tightened my grip to begin the retrieve. But before I could do that, the fly disappeared. Not a splash, or even a swirl, it was more of a drawing-down, an inhalation of the fly by the loch itself. Only the shock prevented me from striking too early. When I lifted the rod tip upwards, after a second's delay, the loch resisted.

There is always a moment after a fish is first hooked when your mind tries to draw together all the evidence it has, to assemble an image of the creature on the end of your line. Sometimes you see it before it takes, so you know, roughly, what you've got. Other times, you just have the weight of it, the strength, on which to make a judgement. I had that weight, that strength, and I had those rumours too. The fish pulled hard. Then harder. I stepped back, got control of the line on the reel, and then I was certain. This was a big trout.

I shouted for Rory, who was still on the other side of the loch. I tried to convey in as few words as possible, as loudly as I could, that he should probably join me. 'Come here now!' I yelled. 'It's *massive!*'

By the time he had reached my side, running and stumbling over heather and soft rush and an old wire fence and boggy, uneven ground, the fish was almost ready to be landed. My nerves, though, were all in pieces. Every time I put pressure on the line, I thought the trout would break it. Every time it jumped or jolted, I feared it was all over. My heart was pounding as the fish hauled against me, the rod tip veering repeatedly towards the water. But it wasn't over. It kept coming, kept getting closer, and when Rory dipped his net into the water, then lifted, it was there. The fish was there.

What we said to each other in that moment I don't recall, but I do remember my surprise at the fact he was carrying a set of digital scales – a gadget I do not possess. He weighed the trout, then subtracted the weight of the net in which it was lying. Four pounds, fourteen ounces: almost twice the size of my previous biggest Shetland brown trout. The rumours, it turned out, were true.

I held the fish in the edge of the loch until it was ready to swim again. It took a moment, then the wide tail pushed hard against my hand and I let it go. I breathed deeply, not quite able to believe that everything had gone to plan, that the fish had been landed and released again. I felt elated, enlivened, and almost unexpectedly pleased with myself. Rory and I are not especially competitive when it comes to fishing, but I must admit I was glad it was me who'd caught this one. I sat down on the heather, trying to take it in, this sense of contented jubilation, of unreasonable euphoria. In those sweet moments of aftermath, the sunset washed everything in golden pink light.

Rory had seen nothing on the other bank. Nothing whatsoever. And so, with that great benevolence one feels after a success, I told him about the first fish – the one I had failed to catch. It might still be there, I said. If you're lucky.

We swapped places. I walked slowly to the other side of the loch, and fished on without real enthusiasm. It didn't seem to matter then if I caught anything else. One fish that size was more than enough for a night.

An hour passed, then another fifteen minutes. The light lingered, but grew weak and thin, until I could barely make out Rory across the loch. Everything felt more effortful, and I was ready to leave. I was satisfied. I packed up my things, then went to sit behind him, on a high bank from where I could safely watch him cast. A fish had been rising on and off, he said, but he couldn't see it any more. He couldn't be sure where it was. His frustration was obvious, and I knew that if I left then he would keep fishing, on into the dark. So I waited a bit longer, watched with him, until . . . 'There!' From where I sat I could see what wasn't clear to him. Twelve metres down the bank, only a few feet from shore, a rise. He cast, following my whispered instructions, and the fly landed perfectly. Another rise, and the trout was on.

Netting a large fish for someone else is more nerve-wracking than netting a large fish for oneself. The consequences of any mistake are potentially worse, and in this case – after Rory had done a flawless job for me – the stakes were even higher. The edge was shallow here, and I had on only walking boots so couldn't step into the water. The trout came in quickly, and seemed determined to beach itself. I lunged at it with the net, but in the poor light I got it wrong. The net touched the fish's head and it flapped on its side in the shallows. I panicked, shifted my position and scooped again. This time it worked.

If you had seen these two fish side by side, you would never have believed they came from the same loch (and almost certainly neither of them had been born in this one). While mine was sparsely spotted and plump, with a distinctly yellow belly, Rory's was thinner, almost silvery, with no red spots at all. It weighed three pounds and fifteen ounces. I would round that up to four, if he would round mine up to five.

I took a photo. It was close to midnight, and though the sky was still pale, there was no real light left to speak of, so I used the flash on my phone's camera. In that stark glare, the trout glistens unnaturally, and my brother looks almost solemn, as if this occasion had been one of the utmost seriousness. Gazing into the lens, with his hands beneath the trout, he looks just like a little boy.

There is a momentousness to the catching of unusually large fish. Deviating far from the norm, as they do, such fish imprint themselves in the memory. They are granted a level of individuality reserved for the scarce, the novel, the truly one-off. They are freaks of the most marvellous kind. It's no wonder that addiction can set in. Like the chasing of rare birds, the pursuit of big fish is a form of thrill-seeking that can easily snowball. One must be followed by another, even larger, even rarer. It's an addiction I'd prefer to avoid.

A few nights later, Rory texted. He was going back to the loch in the hills, he said. Did I want to join him? I thought about it, looked out of the window at the early evening sky, but I didn't have to think for long. I felt no need to return quite so soon. Another time, I said. Maybe next year.

When I woke in the morning, he had texted me a new photograph: a dark, broad brown trout, weighing just over six pounds. He could have had a cast of that fish made and hung it on the wall. Instead, he put it back.

THE
SECRET LOCH

Assynt, 2016

I CAN'T SAY EXACTLY WHERE we were that day, and not just because I'm sworn to secrecy. In fact, the promise I made not to reveal the location of this particular loch was hardly necessary at all, since I'd struggle to find it on a map, let alone remember what it's called.

The name was a Gaelic one, I can say that much, for we were in the northwest of Scotland, in Assynt, where geographical features can be tricky for us monoglots to decipher. I have heard the name spoken only once, and I didn't ask for a translation.

The loch lies high on the shoulder of one of this region's

many mountains, a scree-fringed corrie, sheltered on one side and exposed on every other. In that way, at least, it is just like scores of other scree-fringed corries in this part of the country: an archipelago of clear water, flecked over an ocean of stone. This is a landscape in which everything but that stone can seem small, and in which the world beyond can likewise shrink from thought.

Getting to the loch was not easy. A walk of more than two and a half hours was needed, and at times that walk became a steep, slow trudge that tested my legs and lungs. As we approached the highest point – my friend Will and I, stooped and exhausted – a gust of icy wind hit us square in the face, then failed to die away. Cold rain spattered on our skin, each drop striking like an insult. Down below, it had been a mild spring morning. Up in the mountains, it was still winter. Snow lingered on the rocks above us, and a fringe of thick mist was draped over the crags.

As we huddled on a bank of rock and heather, replenishing ourselves with a packet of cheap flapjacks, it took some effort to recall the enthusiasm with which our day had begun. We were following a tip-off, information given on the condition that it would go no further. The man had told us where to park, and in which direction we should walk. He promised it would be worth the effort, and we believed him. At the time – the night before, in a quiet bar in Ullapool – the fact that he was somewhat drunk had seemed a good thing. Had he been sober, we reasoned, he never would have told us.

Such wishful thinking is difficult to resist, especially

when it comes to rumours like this one, of places known only to a few. These are the places that don't appear in books or on tourist maps, and that no angling guide or tackle shop owner will ever reveal. They are glorious secrets, where the fishing is first rate, and they are found either by exploring or by chasing leads like this one. When we got up that morning, we were counting ourselves lucky. Our half-cut acquaintance had spilled some precious beans, we thought. He had shown us a place we never would have found ourselves. By the time our flapjacks were eaten and our faces were stinging wet with sleet, the sheen had somewhat dimmed on our good fortune.

'Are you thinking what I'm thinking?' I asked, as I unzipped my bag, then took a swig of water to wash down the sugary oats.

Will moved his head from side to side, in a way that didn't make it clear what his thoughts were at all. 'We can't blame him for the weather,' he said, eventually. Which seemed about as fair a judgement as anyone could make.

We set up, turning our backs to the wind, then decided on our starting positions. Will headed off towards the calmest part of the loch, sheltered by a steep corrie wall beyond, and I began more or less where we'd arrived. There was laziness in my decision, I admit, but I prefer to fish with the breeze at my left shoulder, taking slow steps to the right. Casting right-handed, as I do, this gives me maximum flexibility while also making it less likely that I'll take my eye out with a hook.

On that day, however, the wind didn't allow for anything like flexibility. It blustered and buffeted this way and that, at one point lifting a spout of spray and dancing with it across the loch, like a mini tornado. Every few minutes, a gale-force gust would rise and scatter white horses over the surface, making it difficult enough to stand up, let alone cast. All I could do then was to bow my head and wait for it to pass. I spent a lot of time that day with my head down.

Will fishes quite differently from me. He's methodical, choosing the place that looks right to him, then doing everything he can to convince any fish there to take. He'll kneel on the bank to hide himself; he'll scan the water with his polarized glasses; he'll change his flies, his depth, his speed of retrieve. He doesn't give up.

I am not methodical. Not in the slightest. Most times, I tie on a couple of flies that feel right, then cover as much water as I can, trying to find a fish that's willing to take what I'm offering. Sometimes I'll be halfway round a loch before Will's even taken a step.

The two techniques both have their benefits, and I'd say we're about evenly matched, trout for trout. Sometimes – when dry flies are working, for instance – Will tends to do better. My patience will run out before the fish can be persuaded to take. But on other days, luck will be on my side.

On this occasion, dry flies were certainly not needed, but nor was luck much in evidence. I hacked my way down the bank, chucking the line wherever the wind allowed. It was an awkward, clumsy kind of fishing, and it wasn't doing me any good. I saw no fish, no rises, no nothing. My fingers grew cold, and my focus dimmed.

Keeping my flies in the water at all took so much effort that doing it *well* seemed nearly impossible.

When I reached the far end of the loch I crouched behind a boulder to eat my lunch, chewing grimly on my cheese rolls, glad only of the temporary shelter. Peering up towards the opposite end, I could see Will standing exactly where he'd started, but I couldn't make out his face from that distance. I couldn't tell if he looked as miserable as me.

Many anglers keep secrets, that's for sure. But most of them aren't very good ones. There are few parts of the British Isles where one can stumble across a piece of water, full of fish, that is neither private, and therefore out of bounds, nor already well known to others. This part, though, is one of them. There are lochs all over this region that are rarely visited by anglers, and many of them, undoubtedly, offer excellent fishing.

The appeal of such locations is the appeal of almost any secret: the thrill of knowing something that others don't, of finding something that others seek. It is the selfish pleasure of being undisturbed, the ultimate fulfilment of that adolescent yearning for a private space, a wonderland all of one's own.

There is also, I suppose, a dramatic charm to these secrets. A day's fishing can feel like a story unfolding, with suspense, revelation, disappointment and occasionally triumph. Just as in fiction, a secret deepens the drama. And just as in fiction, the trouble, always, is keeping it. A secret is only half as fun if no one knows you've got it, and the temptation to share is ever-nagging. Numerous times, in Shetland, I've been given a name, a hint, a mark on a map, by someone who just couldn't keep the information to themselves any longer. And each time I've been told not to pass it on.

There is always the risk, though, with stories like these, that someone is spinning a tall tale. At best, some minor detail may be falsified or exaggerated. At worst, you can be sent into the hills on a wild trout chase. The risk is amplified, naturally, when that someone is a stranger.

By the time I finished lunch, it took some effort to get going again, to step out from behind my stone. I was in danger of deciding too soon how this story would end, and of making that decision self-fulfilling. I had to find some means to change the course of the day. The waves were lashing on the opposite bank, and there was no hope whatsoever of casting there, so I would need to go back over the same water again. Even *I* recognized the futility of doing so without changing my flies. I swapped both of them – tied on a slim black lure and a scarlet-tailed, weighted nymph – and resumed casting. The wind was in my face now, but at least the rain showers had ceased.

I was nearly back where I'd started when the first fish took, and my concentration had so lapsed by that point that I didn't realize at first what was happening. It was a strange take, fumbling and hesitant, as though the trout couldn't quite make up its mind. But it was on, tussling with the vigour of a much larger fish. It was only half a pound at most, but it was perfect: silvery and freckled, with a narrow yellow stripe along the flank. I unhooked and returned it, grateful and relieved.

Will, it turned out, had caught two by this time, both of them twice the size of mine. I joined him at the lee end of the loch, where he'd stayed, wisely, from the start. Everything there felt calmer and more manageable. Will had no problems casting at all.

As we stood speaking, he looked up and pointed. 'Golden eagle,' he said, directing my eyes to a point high in the crags. The eagle cut slowly through the grey air, effortless and extraordinary. Its great wings turned one way then the other, circling, unflustered by the thumping wind. We watched it for a few moments then parted again. He went to try the side I'd already fished, twice, and I moved on to the windward shore. There, it was a struggle to put the line more than three or four metres out, but I did my best to cover likely spots, casting between gusts, retrieving slowly.

The bottom seemed to fall away close in, and the fish must have been lying at the edge of that drop, searching for food. Despite the struggle to stand, and the laboured, lacklustre casts, I landed first one trout, then another, then missed two more, in less than an hour. Eventually, the wind got the better of me, and I returned to the most sheltered corner, where I netted a fourth and final trout. Each time, it was the red-tailed nymph that succeeded.

It occurred to me that, on a warmer day, a calmer day, this really could be quite a loch. That we'd caught eight good fish between us, despite the conditions, seemed close to miraculous, particularly given my dismal start. I couldn't help but imagine how that warmer, calmer day might turn out, even as I knew that I would likely never return.

We packed away our things and turned to the steep path between boulders down which we would have to scramble. I replayed the long walk up, in reverse, and I thought about the car, two hours or more away, with its heated air and its almost-comfortable seats. I thought about the flapjacks, long eaten, and the flask of coffee, long drunk.

Sometimes, the only good thing about secret places is the fact they're secret. They are a form of currency, the value of which is sustained by *not* spending. In this case, though – a loch so far from where most people are ever likely to venture that keeping it quiet seems almost pointless – there really was something worth keeping quiet about. We were grateful, both of us, to the man who had failed to do so, who had shared this place with strangers for the sheer pleasure of letting us know. Whether he would remember that act of generosity was another matter.

I didn't try to find the loch on a map afterwards, and I didn't ever write down its name. I'm not sure I could even recall where we parked now – which side of which mountain – or the direction that we walked. I'm no good at keeping secrets, to be honest, and there was something rather apt about possessing this one just long enough to enjoy it and no more. We borrowed the secret, and then we let it go.

CAST
FORWARD

WHEN I WAS ABOUT TWENTY years old, a Norwegian musical duo called Kings of Convenience enjoyed some brief popularity in Britain. (Or, quite likely, their popularity lasted longer, but I only took notice briefly.) They were a kind of folk pop band, with songs built around half-whispered harmonies. Imagine Simon and Garfunkel practising in the middle of the night, trying not to wake the neighbours: they sounded something like that. I owned their first album, and for a while I listened to it often. Then, like much of the music of my youth, I put it aside one day and never went back to it. In the two decades that have passed since then, I've forgotten virtually all of those songs. But there's a line that's stuck with me, a fragment that has remained intact. Something about 'the fishing part of fishing'.

What I liked about those words, and what I like still, is that, though they seem to teeter on the edge of nonsense, they also pose an intriguing question. A difficult one, too. After all, fishing is multifaceted. It's about knowledge and expertise, but it's also about chance. It's about freedom and about beauty and about nostalgia. It's about craft and artifice, and about engagement with the natural world. It's about achievement and about humility. It's about fish, obviously, but it's also about people. Given this complexity, then, this multifariousness, given that this hobby is and can be many things at once, what then *is* the fishing part of fishing? Strip away everything that isn't fundamental. What's left?

You wouldn't be too far wrong, I reckon, if you answered *anticipation*. At the heart of this elaborate activity, it seems to me, is the simple act of looking forward.

There is a common misconception among many who have never fished, or who have tried but did not enjoy it, that anglers require patience above all other qualities. The assumption is that, with such meagre and all-too-infrequent rewards for one's time, fishing must demand a near saint-like ability to let hours trundle by without descending into boredom. It must demand a mind without need of stimulation. But nothing could be further from the truth.

The art critic Robert Hughes wrote that, among the ways in which angling had been formative for him, one key lesson had been in 'the craft of handling time'. As a child, he'd had an 'inbuilt impatience'. He wanted, always, 'a fast track from desire to its satisfaction'. But angling does not allow for fast tracks. It can't even promise that you'll get where you want to go. Hughes's lesson, then, as I understand it, was not on the merits of patience. Nothing so banal as that. Rather, it was that pleasure is to be found not only in the achievement of something, but in the expectation of it. It was that submitting to a timescale – or a 'tempo', as he put it – that is not your own, can free you from the need for patience altogether.

Arthur Ransome, the author of *Swallows and Amazons*, was more explicit about this, claiming that patience is the virtue an angler 'least requires'. What is needed instead, he wrote, in a rather lovely turn of phrase, is 'a capacity for prolonged eagerness'. An angler waiting for a fish is no more in need of patience than a football fan waiting for a goal. The fish may be the aim of the game, but the rest is not mere prelude. The rest is what gives meaning to that aim. It is the ultimate source of all the joy.

This isn't to say that an angler is always on the edge of their watery seat. Ransome thought that fishing was 'conducted under continuous tension', but that isn't quite my experience. The tension comes and goes, for me, and it allows for interruption. Perhaps I'm just not as single-minded a fisherman as I ought to be, but I am rarely so intent on what I'm doing that I can't also notice what's going on around me. Noticing, indeed, is part of why I'm there; it is part of the immersion that I seek when I go fishing.

What angling creates, rather, is a feeling that might best be characterized as contented expectation. I spend most of my days fishing just happy to be wherever I am. Though I am always eager to catch fish, I am not dissatisfied so long as the *hope* of catching them remains. The contentment I feel comes from a particular kind of focus, one that allows for taking pleasure in my surroundings, but which pushes out the everyday anxieties, the fears and distractions, the infernal noise of contemporary life. Yet, that focus is predicated on anticipation, on the knowledge that, at any second, something truly wonderful could happen, something that will shatter the spell of my quiet attention. The contentment, paradoxically, is sustained by the desire to end it.

All of the pieces are necessary here. I cannot summon this same feeling, this forward-facing satisfaction, by just sitting outside in a pretty place, enjoyable though that can be. Soon enough, at such times, my mind will drift back to worries that I'd wanted to escape. Without a goal in mind, my thoughts will fill, all too quickly, with the elsewhere. Nor can I summon it, though – and this may surprise some who are not anglers – if the fishing is too easy. When catches come too often, there is no need for hope. It can be exhilarating for a while, certainly, but I have more than once given up on a piece of water because the fish just wouldn't stop biting. When that happens, there is no sense of challenge or achievement, and there is nothing left to look forward to. What's more, the immersive state that angling brings on, the state of 'moment-by-moment attentiveness' and 'blessed self-forgetfulness', as Le Anne Schreiber has described it, just cannot be summoned.

There is a lesson here, perhaps, about the sources of contentment and of joy. Something about the importance of small ambitions, maybe – a fish, after all, is a pretty modest goal in the scheme of things – and of gratification in moderate, unpredictable quantities. Or perhaps it's a mistake to generalize or to extrapolate too far from this particular case. Fishing is a peculiar hobby, a muddle of emotional and practical ingredients that make it incomparable, frankly, to any other activity, except in superficial ways. Perhaps all I can really say is that the fishing part of fishing, the bit that matters most, has something to do with the sensory fullness of one moment and the eager anticipation of the next.

Recently, on an evening in late July, as the sun was going down, Rory and I were in the Loch of Girlsta, the deepest and, by volume, the largest piece of freshwater in Shetland. It's a loch I've never liked much, precisely because of its size. It's always felt unknowable to me, and not in a mysterious or intriguing way. Rather, cold and off-putting. Wherever I happen to start fishing around its banks, on those occasions when I do end up there, I have always been immediately convinced that the fish are at the other side of the loch, or else at the bottom, seventy feet down. It somehow inspires a pessimism that, while not unusual for me at other times, tends to make angling more of a slog.

On this particular evening, however, things were different. We knew the fish were there because we could see them. As the light had begun to fade, late on, what had thus far been a meagre hatch of insects became, at once, a storm. The air filled with tiny, transparent wings, and the surface of the loch was everywhere pocked by the mouths of rising trout. At such times, one gets a sense of just how many fish actually *live* in a loch like this, and of just how often, therefore, one's flies must be seen and ignored by those fish on any given day.

The insects in this case were a species of caenis, a kind of small mayfly that can appear in colossal numbers on warm evenings like this one. For an angler, they can make life difficult – their sheer abundance can trigger a feeding frenzy in which artificial flies may have little success. But as a spectacle, it can be astonishing. When a hatch begins, the air seems no longer clear but filled with a kind of static, a blinking and fluttering of millions of little bodies. These minuscule insects, each no more than a few millimetres long, can obscure the world, like a mist of frantic life.

Mayflies belong to the biological order Ephemeroptera, so called because their existence above water is fleeting, *ephemeral*. After months spent as nymphs, crawling among the rocks and silt on a loch bottom or riverbed, they undergo a transformation, emerging from the water as subimagos, or 'duns', fully winged but not yet sexually mature. Such is the brevity of their airborne existence, however, that their very first act after taking flight is to change yet again, this time to their adult, imago form, known to anglers as 'spinners'. To do this, they land on the ground, in a bush, on a parked car, or indeed on a human being, and shed their skin. In a hatch like this one, the husks of these creatures rapidly amass, covering everything with ghostlike insect forms, abandoned by their owners. Once moulted, the caenis swarm above the water, dancing and mating, before the females deposit their eggs back beneath the surface. In a matter of hours, all of the adults will be dead. Many will be in the stomachs of grateful trout.

As dusk closed in around us, at the side of the loch farthest from the road, I was trying to maintain concentration. My hair, skin and clothes were plastered with thousands of empty insect shucks, and every so often I would pause to brush them off, which only made space for more. All around me, fish were rising. I could see some of them – those within twenty metres, then fifteen – and I could hear others, too. By that time, Rory had more or less disappeared. He had waded out to a small island just offshore, and though I could still hear the swish of his casting, his shape had faded into the gloom. At one point, there was a commotion from where I thought he was standing, some combination of splash or shout, I wasn't sure. 'Everything okay?' I yelled. 'Was it a fish?'

'No,' he called back. 'An otter. He came up next to me and we both got a shock.'

At such times, your ears work harder. They reach out

when your eyes can't do the job. I could see clearly, still, for about the distance I was able to cast. The last light, reflected in the water, helped to keep that space clear. Beyond it, the world was murky, too indistinct for certainty. The shallow-sloping hill behind me, cloaked in heather, had become a dark, undefined mass. If someone had been standing more than a dozen metres back, I might not have seen them. I listened my way into that invisible region, heard sheep calling to each other, heard oystercatchers pleepsing in needless panic, heard splashes from in front of me and barks from somewhere far off, heard movements that I couldn't quite identify – wing beats, perhaps, or feet wading through heather. But all the while I watched, focused on that patch of clear water, where fish were still feeding and were still ignoring my flies.

In a caenis hatch, trout gorge themselves. The food is so plentiful that all they need to do is to cruise close to the surface, scooping the insects up like a whale engulfing plankton. From that position, at the top of the water, their sight, like mine, is limited. They can see only a few inches around their head. (A trout's binocular field of vision is cone-shaped, extending upwards; the deeper they are, the larger the area they can see above.) Catching one, then, is partly a matter of guesswork, of landing your flies where you think a trout is going, and partly a matter of blending in. With so much available to eat, these fish don't need to take chances. They can afford to be certain. Time after time, I would lay my line down in the water, strain my eyes against the dark, only to see a trout veer off in another direction – spooked or distracted, it was impossible to tell. Each cast, I expected things to go differently. I took care, paid attention, watched for the slightest sign of interest, anticipated the swirl in which a hook would disappear, the mouth that would try to make a meal of my fly, the moment when my own eagerness and the fish's would meet.

It was almost midnight when that moment came.

Writing about that evening, remembering it again, I am struck by a kind of mild nostalgia that is, at the same time, the precise opposite: an excitement for the future, for the next occasion. This is a familiar feeling. To recall days spent fishing, no matter how wistfully, is also always to look forward. Where nostalgia is a longing for unrecoverable times and places, this kind of reminiscence carries more ambition. The particular details of a single day can never be repeated, certainly, but the core pleasures, the wonder, the expectation, the curiosity, the satisfaction, are endlessly retrievable. Angling is compulsive precisely because it is predictable in this way. The pleasure is not dependent solely upon results or upon specific circumstances. To remember one fishing trip is to long for another.

This, truly, has been part of the reason for writing this book, is part of the reason always for writing about this subject. It allows me to think about angling even when I'm not able to be beside the water. It means I can bring some of my eagerness home with me, can cultivate it, even. Other angling-adjacent activities serve the same purpose. Fly tying, for instance, or browsing through the websites of fishing tackle manufacturers. Planning trips and poring over maps is good, too, even if those trips never actually happen. Often, I find myself scrolling through anglers' photographs on social media as well, and for much the same reason. A great deal of fishing is done, in other words, when I'm not actually fishing at all.

For me, though, the most consistently enjoyable of these anticipatory acts is reading. After all, why reminisce only about my own angling past when I can read about the experiences of others? Why limit my hopeful daydreaming to waters I already know or am likely to visit? Reading is expansive and restorative. It offers, for this angler, both vicarious adventure and an optimism earned by proxy.

Growing up, I had a drawer packed full of fishing books. The nearest shelves, then, were just outside my bedroom door, but that didn't feel near enough. From charity shops and car boot sales, from friends and generous neighbours, I gathered all the words I could find on the subject and I stacked them in a dresser, suspended between my jumpers and my socks. That drawer was a near-endless source of delight. To open it was to be lifted out into the world. It was to be shown ways of engaging with and being in that world. It was to be promised that my youthful failures, my flailing around in Lerwick Harbour or at the lochside in search of fish, would get me somewhere in the end.

I still read a lot of fishing books, though these days I store them in a more conventional location (mostly in piles around my desk, right now). Even the worst of these books – and there are plenty of bad ones about: pompous, trite, poorly written – offer some scraps of enjoyment. But the best of them can do something special. They convey the experience of particular places, particular times, particular encounters, in such a way as to make those experiences seem almost as vivid and substantial as memory. And at the same time they illuminate and rejuvenate those shared emotions that angling can provide. They make what is new feel familiar and what is familiar feel new. They are generous, also, in the hope they bestow. As I begin to read a fishing book, I am looking forward to knowing what has happened to someone else. As I end it, I am looking forward to what might happen to me.

Angling's ability to induce what is sometimes known as a 'flow state' is one reason for its popularity (even if, as I suspect, few anglers would ever use that language themselves). The combination of repetitive, purposeful movement – especially the repeated casting and false-casting of fly fishing – and a focused, optimistic mindset are both pleasurable and, it turns out, good for your health. In 2021, as part of two regional trials, doctors in the southwest of England and in Manchester began prescribing angling for patients with depression and anxiety. Building on previous studies that have shown increased contact with the natural world to be psychologically as well as physiologically beneficial, the trials will seek to complement or even supplant the use of antidepressants in some patients. The thinking goes that, by generating an immersive and hopeful state of mind, from which worries are dispelled, fishing might be more effective at combatting depression than, say, a daily stroll in the park.

I suspect this is true. I know of no other activity that can concentrate time in quite this way, that can focus one's attention so entirely on the present moment and on the one immediately ahead. The hours I spend fishing are nearly always fret-free – or free, at least, from the kind of fretting that can contribute to psychological distress. Yet, despite this, it is a mistake to imagine angling as a purely escapist, high-spirited hobby, immune from disquiet. It is, after all, a hobby that can cultivate care: care for the places in which one fishes and for the species one likes to catch. That is a benefit of the sport, certainly. But like all care, this one is indivisible from concern.

Angling books often share a rose-tinted view of the past. Their authors recall youthful days, when catches were more prodigious, when rivers and lakes were wilder places, and when fishing offered an encounter with nature that was somehow purer, more meaningful than today. This trend is partly a reflection of the fact that such authors tend to be of a certain age, when the risk of wistful reminiscence is high. But that doesn't mean the view can be dismissed entirely. There is truth to it. To fish throughout a lifetime is to witness a great deal of environmental change, most of which has been for the worse. To pay attention to water, and to what lives within it, is to see damage and diminishment. Nostalgia is one understandable response to this. Another is fear.

The threats to aquatic life today are many and varied. Some are specific, localized threats, such as pollution, while others are global in nature – most notably, climate change. These two strands, however, are not meaningfully separable. Many problems with identifiable local causes are in fact so widespread as to constitute national or international dangers. At the same time, the impacts of global warming are locally particular; they differ by region, by ecosystem, by species. What is faced, then, by the lakes, rivers and oceans that anglers love, is a toxic cocktail of environmental hazards, each one exacerbating and complicating the others.

This cocktail can be clearly observed in one of Britain's most distinctive and important angling habitats. Rising from springs in southern and eastern England, chalk streams are notable for a number of reasons. They are cold, for one thing, and clear, and their natural flow rate – determined by chalk aquifers, rather than just rainfall – tends to be fairly consistent throughout the year. They are, too, alkaline and rich in nutrients, and are perfect habitats for aquatic plants, for insects, and for fish, especially trout. Created as they are by the unique geology of the land from which they emerge, this type of river is globally rare, with the vast majority of them flowing in England. They include some of the most famous fishing rivers in the world: the Test, the Itchen, the Hampshire Avon, the Lea.

Yet their fame and their fecundity has not been enough to spare these waterways from harm. In fact, only a dozen of them, out of 200 or so in Britain, have any kind of specific environmental protection, and a study by the World Wide Fund for Nature in 2014 found that those rivers that were protected were in no better state than those that were not. Overall, fewer than a quarter of chalk streams were found to be in good ecological health, and this may well be an optimistic evaluation.

One of the big problems for chalk streams is that their geographical range corresponds to some of the most densely populated and intensively farmed parts of the country. This means, inevitably, that the long-term needs of the rivers have taken a back seat to the immediate needs of human beings. Chalk streams have for centuries been abused by those who value the land around them. They have been straightened for our convenience, forced to adhere to the lines we draw on maps. They have been rerouted through culverts and tunnels, and buried beneath concrete. Houses, factories and roads have been constructed on their banks.

Rivers can survive this kind of development to a certain extent; they can still host life, even if not to the degree they once did. What they cannot survive, though, is running out of water. And that is exactly the fate of many chalk streams today, some of which are now little more than dry scars in the landscape for much of the year. The primary cause is obvious: the water is going elsewhere. Private water companies abstract colossal quantities from the rivers themselves and from the aquifers that feed them, mostly for domestic use. In some cases, such as the Cam, which flows through Cambridge, those companies then pump additional water from the aquifers back into the rivers, in order to mitigate (or disguise) the problem, while at the same time making it worse. All of this is likely compounded by changing rainfall patterns in winter, caused by climate change, which is failing to adequately replenish the groundwater.

In addition to what is being taken out, these rivers are also suffering because of what is being put in. Agricultural run-off is one problem, with excess phosphorus from fertilizers triggering algal blooms and eutrophication, which can choke the life from water. Industrial waste is also an issue. Salad-washing facilities, for instance, have been caught discharging pesticides, including neonicotinoids, into chalk streams, destroying insect life downstream in the process. Perhaps the most significant pollution threat of all, though, is from sewage, which is currently released into rivers in extraordinary quantities. In 2020 alone, water companies were found to have discharged untreated sewage into English waters for a total of 3.1 million hours. And though the problem varies by region and by waterway, there is nowhere that is unaffected. In that same year, not a single one of England's rivers was found to have good chemical status. Not one. According to the former singer turned environmental activist Feargal Sharkey, 'England's rivers have become nothing more than an extension of the sewage system, polluted, poisoned and exploited for profit.'

Together, these issues present a daunting prospect to anyone who values chalk streams as healthy, thriving ecosystems. No single perpetrator can be identified. No single solution can make the kind of difference that is needed. Those who are guilty of inflicting the various forms of damage on these rivers rely on the number of people who notice or who care being small. They rely on indifference from the public and from government in order to continue getting away with it, and for the most part indifference is what they get. A handful of community groups and environmental charities have been persistent in their efforts to protect these waters, and anglers and their representatives have been especially active. But despite some local successes – a clean-up here, a prosecution there – it's hard not to conclude that without radical change these rivers will continue to decline. Their reputation among anglers can be propped up by the stocking of hatchery-bred trout, but only to a certain extent. Without major ecological improvement, that reputation is likely to appear increasingly hollow. It may become just another form of nostalgia.

In some parts of the world, the threat to fish is so great, and its potential consequences so enormous, that to consider the impact on angling and anglers at all is to fundamentally miss the point. In the Pacific Northwest of North America, for instance, populations of Pacific salmon have been sharply declining for years, and the numbers of certain species in certain river systems are now approaching collapse. This is an economic problem, of course, since angling and related recreational activities bring money to this region, and it's an inconvenience to people who like to fish for these species. But those immediate issues are dwarfed by the wider environmental disaster that this decline undoubtedly spells. For here's the problem: The ecosystems of the Pacific Northwest – its rainforests, rich with life – are sustained by salmon. Returning in huge numbers from the ocean in order to breed in freshwater, their bodies packed with marine nutrients, every one of these salmon will die, thereby depositing those nutrients into the very waters in which they themselves were born.

To take just one example from within this enormous area, it's estimated that, prior to the twentieth century, well over ten million Chinook salmon returned to the Columbia River system in Washington State each year. Those millions of fish in turn fed many millions of other animals and birds, from iconic species, such as bears, wolves and eagles, right down to the smallest of creatures, and ultimately to the forests themselves. Trees in this region have been shown to derive up to 75 per cent of their nitrogen from salmon. The life of this entire region, then, relies on their presence. Without them, everything suffers. Yet, today, that run of more than ten million fish is estimated to be as low as 200,000 per year, and falling.

The causes of this disaster are not a mystery, but nor are they easy to solve. Habitat loss and degradation are, as usual, part of the problem, both along the coast, where salmon spend most of their lives, and on the rivers themselves. As the human population increases, so too does the pressure on its wildlife. Some of that pressure is incremental – development along riverbanks, for instance – but there are specific impediments too, such as culverts and dams, which can prevent fish from swimming upstream. Then there is climate change, which impacts fish in a multitude of ways. First, the temperature of rivers is rising, and salmon cannot survive in warm water. Second, flooding and wildfires are becoming more regular occurrences, and both can be devastating to young fish. Third, the food on which salmon live while in the ocean – plankton, crustaceans and smaller fish species – are themselves growing less numerous. Changes at the bottom of the food chain are echoing all the way to the top.

As these various threats have grown, others have joined them. Commercial fishing, for instance, was not a problem while stocks were healthy, but as the numbers of salmon fall, the relative impact of that fishing rises exponentially. Likewise, natural predators can begin to have a seriously detrimental effect, especially if their own diets are being knocked out of balance by the same environmental changes. Some predators, such as sea lions, are now targeting and eating salmon more than ever before. Others, like orcas, are themselves disappearing. It is a complex, muddled story of decline, and it's hard to know what can actually be done about it. It's hard to know where to even start.

Not every species of salmon has been as badly affected as Chinook, and not every river has been as badly affected as the Columbia. But the damage is happening everywhere, from Oregon and Washington State, through British Columbia, to Alaska. It is an environmental catastrophe within which, frankly, angling is of little importance. But anglers are. They are among those who see these changes first-hand, who recognize these threats and who fear them. Anglers can be – *ought* to be – among those who shout loudest about what is happening, who insist, even in the face of others' indifference, that fish matter.

'What a beautiful world it was once,' the narrator of Norman Maclean's *A River Runs Through It* declares. 'At least a river of it was.' Such immense sadness is contained in those lines.

Fishing is a way of reminding myself that the world is still beautiful. It is a way of confronting myself – and comforting myself – with that fact. But to stand beside water today is also to be confronted by loss, by the ways in which we have made and are making this world uglier. It is to see flocks of plastic bags, slung from trees and fence posts, pressed into corners by oblivious winds and currents. It is to see broken glass and beer cans, abandoned by those who enjoyed a place but who had no compunctions about causing it harm. It is to witness what should not be there. Last week, I watched as contaminated water from an abandoned mine poured into the river in which I was fishing. A near-fluorescent plume of orange extended many metres from the outflow, and for a long distance downstream the riverbed was coated with rust-coloured gunk. Yesterday, elsewhere on that same river, and miles from any town, I waded into a pool and nearly tripped on a running shoe that was wedged between rocks. Beside it: what looked like an old, upturned shopping basket.

Such needless damage is impossible to ignore. You can find it more or less everywhere. But it amounts, ultimately, to a lesser threat than that which cannot be seen on a single trip, that which is noticeable only over an extended period. For anglers, the global decline in insect numbers and diversity is surely among the most significant of these changes (a decline which itself has multiple causes). While there is regional variation in this trend, it is thought that numbers of at least 40 per cent of insect species worldwide are now falling, with a third of species endangered. A review of global data found an overall decline of more than 2.5 per cent per year, while a recently published study undertaken in Germany identified a staggering 76 per cent drop in total insect biomass over the previous twenty-seven years. It is impossible that declines like this have not already affected wild fish populations, and impossible that they will not continue to do so. Fewer insects means fewer fish, it really is as simple as that.

This is, still, a beautiful world, and I am more conscious of that fact when fishing than at almost any other time. But human beings are certainly doing their damnedest to make it otherwise. To pay attention to the places one loves, or even just to pay attention to the news, is to feel a kind of dread about the threats this world is facing. Everything, it seems, is always getting worse.

Or almost everything.

I have mentioned more than once in this book the fact that many rivers in the UK and elsewhere are actually in a better state today than they were in the mid-twentieth century. This is true. The Industrial Revolution was a disaster for aquatic life. For centuries, there were few restrictions on what people could dump in our waterways. Sewage, detergents, industrial dyes, coal-mining effluent, ammonia, oil. For those rivers unfortunate enough to flow anywhere near our towns and cities, most of what we didn't need would ultimately end up in their water. It's no wonder that many of those rivers were for decades entirely dead. Nothing could live in them so long as the pollution continued to flow.

But rivers are pretty good at cleaning themselves up, given the chance. Once restrictions were put in place, and once those restrictions were policed, the water grew cleaner. Life – and fish – returned.

To note this improvement is not to minimize or to distract from the bad news. It is merely to demonstrate that things can change, they can improve. Seventy years ago, nobody would have imagined that a healthy population of salmon would return to the River Clyde. Nobody would have imagined that the Thames could become a clean river again. This fact is worth bearing in mind when considering the problems that our waters face today. For while the challenges are enormous, that is not a reason for inaction. The unimaginable, sometimes, can come to pass.

I must admit that I am not an optimist when it comes

to climate change, or to environmental damage more widely. I'm not much of an optimist about anything really, except perhaps fishing. Which is the point, I suppose. Or one of the points. It's what I get from all this, in the end. It's what is renewed over and over when I look for fish. It's hope. Hope and hope and hope. Cast and cast and cast.

THE FORTH
AND CLYDE CANAL

North Lanarkshire, 2020

A FEW WEEKS HAD PASSED since Roxani and I took our walk along the Forth and Clyde Canal. In that time, the weather had turned colder and I had turned forty. (These changes were not related, though there were mornings when I wondered if they might be.) I had known all along that I would go back there to fish. The thought of it had been pestering me, the thought of what might be there, beneath the surface. But I waited, allowing the anticipation to build, until a day that felt just right.

I'd read a little about fly fishing for coarse species in the meantime, though nothing that filled me with confidence. Almost any fish, I'd learned, could be caught with a fly, but there were a lot of caveats. For one thing, my research suggested that winter was entirely the wrong time to be trying this. The fish would feed more enthusiastically once things warmed up. For another thing, I could find no consensus at all on the kinds of flies that I ought to be using. As so often in angling, lots of people had opinions, and nearly all of them were different.

I parked alongside a lock, in a gravel car park just large enough for three vehicles. It was a few miles east of where we'd walked before, and I hoped it might be quieter there, away from the main road. I put a spool of line and a box of flies in my pocket, grabbed the rod and reel, and hung a landing net on my belt. I set out along the towpath with my head down, eager to make a start. But I didn't get far.

A short distance beyond the lock, on a stone platform jutting out into the canal, was an old man fastened by a lead to an old dog. The man had his back to the path, and seemed to be looking at a family of swans in the water below. But that was just a ruse. In fact, he was lying in wait for company.

As I neared, the man turned round to face me, muttered a greeting, then let his eyes fall to the fishing rod in my hand. The dog – a scraggy-looking thing, half-spaniel at best – appeared to mirror his movements. It too spun round, looked up at me, then down, then up again.

'A fly rod?' the man asked (which was well deduced, since the reel was not yet attached).

'Yup,' I nodded, hoping I could keep things short.

The man told me that he had just taken up fly fishing a couple of months before, after someone gave him a broken rod, which he'd repaired. The man was seventy-five, maybe eighty years old, which is as good an age to start as any, I suppose.

We chatted for a few minutes. He explained, with the tone of a patient teacher, that I'd be better off taking my fly rod to the trout fishery up the road. I agreed that I probably would. 'But since I'm here,' I said, turning back towards the path, 'I might as well . . .'

'Have you ever eaten a pike?' he asked then, blocking my conversational escape route entirely. I breathed out, shook my head and admitted that I hadn't. 'Fellow told me they were good eating,' he said. 'Lots of bones, but . . .' He shrugged. 'I was thinking, next year, I might go up to the Lake of Menteith, get a wee pike and pop it in the smoker. Never know, might be the best fish I've ever tasted.'

I was pretty certain that killing pike was not allowed at the Lake of Menteith, but that didn't seem the right moment to mention it. And anyway, he was still talking.

'I ate a fish once,' he said, 'in South Africa. Most beautiful white flesh. Best I'd ever had. Next day, I went out to try and find it in the shop. You wouldn't believe it. Ugliest looking thing you could imagine. Some kind of eel, it was, I think.' He looked at me, as though to gauge my response, and I tried to appear shocked and impressed at the same time. 'Problem with us,' he went on, 'is we eat with our eyes.'

This may have been a well-rehearsed remark, but it was a good one nonetheless. I nodded, to show my appreciation for his insight, and to suggest, at once, that this piece of wisdom might be the ideal closing point for our conversation, the pinnacle from which we could both descend and go our separate ways. I waited a second or two to see if he felt the same, and when I suspected that he might, I made my move.

'Well,' I said, 'let's just see how it goes.'

I turned and headed west along the towpath.

'Have a good day,' he called out, his little dog adding a bark of its own.

I raised my hand and waved. 'You too,' I said.

The canal, on that stretch, was lined with reeds and dried bulrushes, their flower spikes like fat cigars impaled on skewers. Here and there, a space had been scraped out for anglers, just a narrow gap in the vegetation, with a flattened spot on the bank above. I passed half a dozen of these, then ten, then twelve, waiting for some kind of sign that I'd found the right place to begin. Something that said 'fish'. I kept on walking until, eventually, I realized I was just putting it off, and that I would have to make a decision. At the next space in the rushes, I stepped down off the path to the muddy bank below, and began to thread the fly line through the rod.

When it came to flies, I hedged my bets and picked two. The first was a tiny grey shrimp pattern, chosen because of its size, and the fact it was slightly weighted, which would carry it towards the bottom. And chosen, too, because it looked to all intents and purposes like a maggot, which was what any sensible angler would be using for bait. That one, I thought, should work for any of the smaller species that might be here. The second fly was a black sparkly lure, which would imitate a baby fish. It was big enough that it might appeal to a hungry perch, but too small, I thought, to interest a pike. My tippet was thin, and a pike would break it with ease.

At the last moment, I tied on a third fly – a big, bushy sedge – at the very top end of the tippet. That one was chosen less for its attractive qualities than for its buoyancy. Having forgotten to bring with me the bright bite indicators that would have made things simpler, this fly would act, essentially, as a float, with the other two dangling beneath it. Enticingly, I hoped.

I cast the whole lot out, just to the left of where I was standing, gave a few tweaks of the line to help the lower flies sink, then waited. I'd read that very little movement was required, so I let the flies sit, just twitching them occasionally in case that triggered a bite. I watched the sedge move slowly towards the lily pads along the bank.

It occurred to me that this was the first time I had deliberately cast for coarse fish since I was sixteen years old. Since the day my father died, in fact. On that hot afternoon in Sussex, so far oblivious to what had happened, I caught tench (two of them, if I remember right, though it's possible I don't). Afterwards, I packed away my ugly fibreglass rod – the one I'd bought with my uncle eight years previously, the one that had accompanied me through my childhood summers – and I never used it again. In a lifetime of angling, there are currents and eddies. There are sudden changes of direction. There are memories that rise, unbidden, to the surface.

I cast again, a little farther this time, and allowed the floating sedge to drift. There was almost no wind, just a gust now and again, so the fly's movement was eccentric and unpredictable. It would swing one way, spin, then return to where it began. I let it sit a while, then raised the rod, flicked it towards the centre of the canal, and kept watching. My vision softened gradually from that hand-made fly to the reflection in which it sat, from the clutch of hook-bound deer hair to the bare trees on the opposite bank, which were doubled in the water. At one point, an odd movement there, a narrow flash of white beside my fly, became a real, living deer, browsing among those same trees. Only its pale back end was visible, and a scrap of bronze on its flank. Minutes later, turning on one of those hunches that have no cause you can name, I saw another deer, a young one, asleep on the rough ground behind me. It was curled up between bushes, certain of its own invisibility. I took another cast, then turned again, and sure enough the deer had vanished.

I walked along the towpath towards the next space, back in the direction from which I'd arrived. Moving often, I'd read, offered the best chance of success. Coarse anglers can throw handfuls of bait into the water to attract fish to where they are, but fly anglers don't have that luxury. They need to go looking. So I moved, then moved again.

In the rowan trees on the other side of the path, long-tailed tits were likewise moving, skittering from branch to branch in search of food, chatting to each other all the while. On the far side of the canal, coots were feeding too. Their terse burps erupted from within the weeds, though the birds themselves stayed mostly hidden. There was a jostling all around me in that place, a toing and froing in almost every direction. There was a busy road some distance behind me, and the train line between Glasgow and Edinburgh was up on the hill ahead. There were fluorescent-clad cyclists pinging their bells along the towpath. There were elderly couples, arm in arm. There were mallards, cruising. There were little planes coming in to land, at an airstrip not far away. There were robins scuttling in the undergrowth. There were intermittent gusts of wind. There were wings and feet and branches and wheels.

When I fish, I am leaning towards stillness. By which I don't mean the absence of movement, but rather the quieting of unwanted distractions. It is a state of selective attunement that, most often, returns to me easily. But on this day I was failing. The world clamoured for attention. It prodded at me constantly. Even my own body was at it. My fingers ached and shivered with the cold; my stomach scolded me for neglecting to bring lunch.

A smattering of rain began to fall, proving the forecast wrong, and I pulled my hood up over my head. I fished my way back along the path towards the car, sometimes stopping in one spot for just a moment, sometimes casting carefully, taking my time. On one retrieve, I paused before lifting the flies, and a fish nosed the surface just in front of me. My heart rate jumped, and I stopped, let the line sit a moment longer, tweaking, tweaking, tweaking, waiting for it to take. I ran through the list of candidates in my head, the species it could possibly be. I imagined the fish as a perch, rough-scaled and camouflage-striped, its spiny dorsal fin aloft. Or else a roach, with its bright silver body, fringed with scarlet. Or perhaps a rudd, all golden and plump and glum. I imagined these fish that I hadn't seen or held in years, and I wanted, urgently, to see them all again. I waited, waited, cast again and waited, but nothing came. Whatever it was did not return.

By mid-afternoon, I was back in sight of the lock. The canal is narrower there and I could cast almost to the opposite bank. The rain turned, for a time, into sleet, and a family of mute swans cruised up to meet me, thinking I was throwing bread. I hissed at them, urging them to move on, and when they refused, I moved myself.

I'd seen no more signs of fish at all, just that one meagre glimpse. I was almost ready to call it a day, to pack the rod away and go home, to put the heating on and open a pack of biscuits, to declare my return to the canal, and to coarse fish, a failure. I walked with my eyes on the water, let two joggers pass me on the towpath, then turned on to the stone platform where I'd met the old man and his dog a few hours earlier.

One last cast, I told myself. One last cast.

I stood at the corner farthest from the lock and flicked the line towards the other bank, to a sheltered spot that looked like it could hold fish. Or the chance of fish, anyway. The hope of them.

The flies landed where I wanted them to go. The lower

two sank, leaving only the sedge visible on the surface, a speck of something my own hands had made. I watched it closely, waiting for the tremble that might be evidence of life below. One tweak, then wait again.

As I watched, the light around me shifted, and the reflection of a tree bloomed into being, eclipsing the clump of deer hair and fur in the water. A patch of blue sky emerged then, not above but below, transforming the surface, saturating it, as though everything around me might also be found there, if only I looked carefully enough. In that moment, the fly returned to focus, suspended between reflection and expectation. I leaned towards the water, and I tightened my fingers on the line.

GLOSSARY

BARBLESS HOOKS Traditionally, most hooks had a tiny barb near the point to help hold fish more securely. Because these barbs can harm fish that are returned alive, many people today use hooks without them.

BLOB A very simple artificial fly pattern that resembles a colourful ball of fluff.

BOBBIN HOLDER A tool used to hold and dispense thread for tying flies.

BUZZER An artificial fly that imitates an emerging midge.

COARSE FISH All freshwater species in the UK are known as *coarse fish*, except trout, salmon, char and grayling, which are classed as game fish. (Grayling have been inconsistently categorized over the years, and many anglers still consider them to be *coarse fish*. Taxonomically, however, they are salmonids, and therefore game fish.)

CREEL A wicker basket used for carrying fish.

COVER To *cover* a piece of water is to cast flies to it, or retrieve them through it, so that any fish there are likely to have seen those flies.

DROPPER When fishing with two or more flies at once, a *dropper* is a small section of line tied partway up the *tippet*, to which the additional fly is attached.

DRY FLY An artificial fly that floats on the surface.

EMERGER An artificial fly that hangs from the surface film, or just below it, to imitate an insect in the process of *hatching*.

FALSE CAST When *fly fishing*, a *false cast* is one in which the line remains suspended in the air, without landing on the water. *False casts* can be used to add length to the line and thus to cast farther.

FISHERY Usually, a piece of water into which fish are stocked for the benefit of anglers.

FLY FISHING A form of angling in which artificial flies are used to attract fish, and in which no weight – other than the line itself – is required for casting.

FLY LINE The thick and relatively heavy line that makes fly casting possible. Originally constructed from silk, most *fly lines* are now made of plastic.

FOUL HOOKED A fish that is caught on any part of the body other than the lips or mouth is said to be *foul hooked*.

GOLDHEAD An artificial fly with a metal head – often brass or tungsten – that helps it to sink quickly.

HACKLE A feather turned around the body of a fly, creating a collar of protruding feather barbs.

HACKLE PLIERS The tool with which a feather is turned around a fly to create a *hackle*.

HATCH When an insect emerges and takes flight from the surface of the water, it is said to have *hatched*. When many insects are emerging from the water at once, it is known collectively as a *hatch*.

HATCHERY Fish are artificially bred and reared in a *hatchery* (sometimes known as a fish farm).

INDICATOR A small buoyant object fixed to the *leader* or *tippet*, which can show – by its sudden disappearance – that a fish has taken.

LEADER In *fly fishing*, the *leader* is the section of line that is attached to the end of the *fly line*. It is usually tapered and concludes with a *tippet*, to which the flies are attached.

LURE An artificial fly that imitates a small fish.

MISS A fish that strikes at a fly or bait but is not hooked is said to have been *missed*.

NYMPH Aquatic insect larvae, and the artificial fly patterns intended to imitate those larvae.

NYMPHING The various fly-fishing techniques – among them French and Czech – by which artificial *nymphs* are fished, especially along the bottom of a river.

PRIEST A small cosh used to kill fish.

PUT-AND-TAKE A label applied to waters in which fish are regularly stocked for anglers to catch and take home.

RISE When a fish takes an insect from the water's surface, it is known as a *rise*. The term also refers to the evidence of this feeding behaviour – often a series of concentric circles – as seen from above.

SEDGE The adult caddisfly.

STREAMER An artificial fly that imitates a small fish.

TACKLE UP To get ready to begin fishing.

TAIL FLY When fishing with more than one fly at once, the *tail fly* is the one attached to the very end of the line.

TIPPET In *fly fishing*, the *tippet* is the piece of line to which the fly or flies are attached. It is always the thinnest segment, at the end – or tip – of the line.

VICE The tool in which hooks are held when tying flies.

WET FLY A generic term for artificial flies that sink. More specifically, it can refer to certain traditional patterns from, for instance, Scotland and Ireland.

NOTES

The following sources are those quoted or referred to in the text, but many other works informed the writing of this book. Among them, Tom Fort's social history of angling in Britain, *Casting Shadows* (William Collins, 2020), and Andrew Herd's history of fly fishing, *The Fly* (Medlar Press, 2003), were especially useful. Jen Corrinne Brown's *Trout Culture* (University of Washington Press, 2015) taught me a great deal about the place of fly fishing in American history and culture, and Bob Wyatt's *What Trout Want* (Stackpole Books, 2013) provided expert corroboration of my own amateur hunches about fly patterns and fish 'selectivity'.

INTRODUCTION

5   '*fishing is the activity . . .* ': Jim Harrison, 'Older Fishing', in *Astream: American Writers on Fly Fishing*, ed. Robert DeMott (Skyhorse Publishing, 2014), p. 105.

6   '*fishing is folly . . .* ': Ailm Travler, 'Fly Fishing Folly', in *Uncommon Waters: Women Write About Fishing*, ed. Holly Morris (The Seal Press, 1991), p. 208.

7   '*No life, my honest scholar . . .* ': Izaak Walton and Charles Cotton, *The Compleat Angler* (Arcturus Publishing, 2010), p. 72.

7   '*the most honest . . .* ': ibid., p. 23.

7   '*men of mild . . .* ': ibid., p. 29.

10 '*I write about fly fishing . . .* ': W. D. Wetherell, *One River More*, in *A River Trilogy* (Skyhorse Publishing, 2018), p. 653.

SCALAND WOOD

15   *'small stillnesses . . .'*: Ted Leeson, *The Habit of Rivers:
      Reflections on Trout Streams and Fly Fishing* (The Lyons
      Press, 2006), p. 1.

16   *'all anglers are still children'*: Chris Yates, *The Deepening Pool*
      (The Medlar Press, 2005), p. 14.

A FLEETING THING

22   *'You become the fish . . .'*: Tracy K. Smith, 'Astral', in *Duende*
      (Graywolf Press, 2007), p. 27.

26   *'If there can be said . . .'*: A. Laurence Wells, *The Observer's
      Book of Freshwater Fishes of the British Isles* (Frederick
      Warne & Co., 1961), p. 46.

26   *'a hell of a lot . . .'*: John Gierach, *Trout Bum* (Simon &
      Schuster Paperbacks, 1986), p. 7.

30   *'The real truth about fly-fishing . . .'*: John Gierach, *Another
      Lousy Day in Paradise* (Simon & Schuster Paperbacks, 1996),
      p. 223.

31   *'picking up God's rhythms'*: Norman Maclean, *A River Runs
      Through It and Other Stories* (University of Chicago Press,
      2001), p. 2.

31   *'To him, all good things . . .'*: ibid., p. 4.

31   *'a halo of himself'*: ibid., p. 20.

31–2 *'iridescent with . . .'*: ibid., p. 21.

32   *'The canyon was glorified . . .'*: ibid., p. 22.

32   '*"I've told you all I know . . ."*': ibid., p. 103.

THE IMITATION OF LIFE

54   *'the black spot . . .'*: Izaak Walton and Charles Cotton, *The
      Compleat Angler*, pp. 183–4.

57–8 Quotes from Ælian, *De Natura Animalium*, are as translated in William Radcliffe, *Fishing from the Earliest Times* (John Murray, 1921), pp. 187–8.

65 '*A trout fly . . .*': Ted Leeson, *Jerusalem Creek: Journeys into Driftless Country* (The Lyons Press, 2004), p. 210.

KEEP OUT!

76 '*you must not . . .*': from Alfred Duggan's modern English translation of *A Treatyse of Fysshynge wyth an Angle*, published in *Sports Illustrated*, 20 May 1957, p. 79.

77 '*to promote the participation . . .*': Richard C. Hoffmann, 'Fishing for Sport in Medieval Europe: New Evidence', *Speculum* 60 (4), 1985, p. 900.

77 '*idle persons . . .*': from Alfred Duggan's modern English translation of *A Treatyse of Fysshynge wyth an Angle*, published in *Sports Illustrated*, 20 May 1957, p. 79.

82 '*social control*': Alison Locker, 'The Social History of Coarse Angling in England AD 1750–1950', *Anthropozoologica* 49 (1), 2014, p. 102.

83 *A survey of around 2,400 UK anglers*: Paul Stolk, 'Angling Participation: Interim Report', Angling Research Resources, 2009.

84 *the National Angling Survey*: Adam Brown, 'The National Angling Survey', Angling Research Resources, 2012.

84 *a 2016 US government report*: 'National Survey of Fishing, Hunting, and Wildlife-Associated Recreation', U.S. Department of the Interior, Fish and Wildlife Service, and U.S. Department of Commerce, U.S. and Census Bureau, 2006.

85 *a more recent survey*: 'Special Report on Fishing', Outdoor Foundation, 2018.

86 '*the fastest trout-fly tier in the nation*': 'Fly Tier', *The New Yorker*, 23 May 1942, p. 9.

86   '*the Fabergés of the fishing world*': David Profumo, quoted in
      Anna Tyzack, 'Megan Boyd: The Scottish Fishing Fly Maker
      Who Wove Magic', *The Telegraph*, 4 February 2014.

92   '*Provide child care . . .*': Kate Fox, 'Life Among the Anglish',
      in *Astream: American Writers on Fly Fishing*, ed. Robert
      DeMott (Skyhorse Publishing, 2014), pp. 87–8.

94   '*safety and community . . .*': Beth Collier, 'Black Absence in
      Green Spaces', *The Ecologist*, 10 October 2019.

IN THE WAY OF WILDNESS

122   '*the deep ache . . .*': Harry Middleton, *The Bright Country*
      (Pruett Publishing Company, 2000), p. 132.

123   '*For sheer grandeur . . .*': Negley Farson, *Going Fishing*
      (Hamlyn Paperbacks, 1983), p. 64.

123   '*the further away . . .*': Negley Farson, *The Way of a
      Transgressor* (Zenith, 1983), p. 25.

130   '*Two plus two . . .*': Anders Halverson, *An Entirely Synthetic
      Fish: How Rainbow Trout Beguiled America and Overran the
      World* (Yale University Press, 2010), p. 121.

135   '*the most concentrated . . .*': Jim Hunter, quoted in Kevin
      McKenna, 'Scotland Has the Most Inequitable Land
      Ownership in the West. Why?', *The Observer*, 10 August
      2013.

136   '*in a world . . .*': Matthew L. Miller, *Fishing Through the
      Apocalypse: An Angler's Adventures in the 21st Century* (The
      Lyons Press, 2019), p. 208.

137   '*about looking for . . .*': Charles Rangeley-Wilson, *The
      Accidental Angler* (Yellow Jersey Press, 2007), p. 27.

PUTTING BACK AND TAKING AWAY

152–3 '*imagine using worms . . .*': Jack Turner, quoted in Ted
      Kerasote, *Heart of Home: People, Wildlife, Place* (Villard
      Books, 1997), p. 108.

153   *biologists at the Roslin Institute*: L. U. Sneddon, V. A. Braithwaite and M. J. Gentle, 'Do Fishes Have Nociceptors? Evidence for the Evolution of a Vertebrate Sensory System', *Proceedings of the Royal Society of London: Biological Sciences* 270, 2003.

154   *'neither their rationale . . .'*: J. D. Rose, R. Arlinghaus, S. J. Cooke, B. K. Diggles, W. Sawynok, E. D. Stevens and C. D. L. Wynne, 'Can Fish Really Feel Pain?', *Fish and Fisheries* 15 (1), 2014, p. 125.

158   *'A thing is right . . .'*: Aldo Leopold, *A Sand County Almanac: And Sketches Here and There* (Oxford University Press, 1968), pp. 224–5.

161–2 *'normal mammalians . . .'*: ibid., p. 408.

162   *Peter Singer's book*: Peter Singer, *Animal Liberation* (Avon Books, 1975).

162   *'merely as means'* and *'inherent value'*: Tom Regan, *The Case for Animal Rights* (Routledge, 1988), p. 181, p. 241.

162   *'is an individual . . .'*: Joan Dunayer, 'Animal Equality', a speech given at the Austrian Animal Rights Conference, 2002.

163   *'It is in the nature . . .'*: Roger Scruton, *Animal Rights and Wrongs* (Metro Books, 2000), p. 55.

169   *'A peasant becomes fond . . .'*: John Berger, *About Looking* (Pantheon, 1980), p. 5.

170   *'inclined to embrace . . .'*: Jeff McMahan, 'The Meat Eaters', *The New York Times*, 19 September 2010.

171   *'There is no death . . .'*: Gary Snyder, *The Practice of the Wild* (Shoemaker & Hoard, 2003), p. 196.

171   *'have the power . . .'*: Robin Wall Kimmerer, *Braiding Sweetgrass: Indigenous Wisdom, Scientific Knowledge and the Teachings of Plants* (Milkweed Editions, 2013), p. 36.

173   *'I have thought . . .'*: Annie Dillard, *Teaching a Stone to Talk: Expeditions and Encounters* (Perennial Library, 1988), p. 64.

THE POSSIBILITY OF MONSTERS

193 *'For half an hour . . .'*: Ernest Hemingway, 'On the Blue Water', *Esquire*, 1 October 1973.

194 *'There is not another strength . . .'*: Lorian Hemingway, 'The Young Woman and the Sea', in *Uncommon Waters: Women Write About Fishing*, ed. Holly Morris (The Seal Press, 1991), p. 45.

194 *'wholesale slaughter . . .'*: ibid., p. 50.

197 *One can find a richer experience*: Nan Shepherd, *The Living Mountain* (Canongate, 2011).

CAST FORWARD

218 'the fishing part of fishing': Eirik Glambek Bøe and Erlend Øye, Kings of Convenience, 'Singing Softly to Me', from *Quiet is the New Loud* (EMI, 2001).

218 *'the craft of handling time . . .'*: Robert Hughes, *A Jerk on One End: Reflections of a Mediocre Fisherman* (The Harvill Press, 2000), p. 8.

219 *'least requires . . .'*: Arthur Ransome, *Rod and Line* (Oxford Paperbacks, 1980), p. 45.

221 *'moment-by-moment attentiveness . . .'*: Le Anne Schreiber, 'Life After Fly Fishing', in *Astream: American Writers on Fly Fishing*, ed. Robert DeMott (Skyhorse Publishing, 2014), p. 246.

230 *a study by the World Wide Fund for Nature*: Rose O'Neill and Kathy Hughes, 'The State of England's Chalk Streams', WWF-UK, 2014.

231 *'England's rivers . . .'*: Feargal Sharkey, quoted in 'Dumping Raw Sewage in Rivers', *Salmon & Trout Conservation* blog, 1 April 2021.

235 *'What a beautiful world . . .'*: Norman Maclean, *A River Runs Through It*, p. 56.

236   *A review of global data*: Francisco Sánchez-Bayo and Kris A. G. Wyckhuys, 'Worldwide Decline of the Entomofauna: A Review of Its Drivers', *Biological Conservation* 232, April 2019.

236   *a recently published study*: Caspar A. Hallmann, Martin Sorg, Eelke Jongejans, Henk Siepel, Nick Hofland, Heinz Schwan, Werner Stenmans, et al., 'More than 75 Percent Decline over 27 Years in Total Flying Insect Biomass in Protected Areas', *PLOS One* 12 (10), October 2017.

ACKNOWLEDGEMENTS

Most of my fishing these days is done alone, but that hasn't always been the case. Over the years, I've learned from and enjoyed the company of many other anglers. I was fortunate, especially in my teenage years, to be encouraged – and put up with – by numerous members of Shetland Anglers Association. I'm inordinately grateful for that, and to Alec Miller in particular, who has been a generous fishing companion for three decades now. In recent years, I've enjoyed my all-too-infrequent angling trips with Will Miles, and I'm thankful to him not just for his company on those occasions, but for allowing me to write about two of them in this book.

Though she doesn't fish herself (yet?), Roxani Krystalli often accompanies me by the water, and those days, like all time spent with her, are enriched by her presence. Roxani is also my first and best reader, and every chapter in this book has been improved by her comments, her questions and her endless curiosity.

My brother, Rory Tallack, also read these chapters as they were written and offered suggestions and corrections along the way. Rory appears often in these pages – he was there on that very first fishing trip, and he has been there so often since – and it is only right that this book is dedicated to him.

Neither of my parents ever had the slightest interest in fishing, but both of them helped to keep my youthful obsession alive. They regularly drove me to various lochs and lakes, in Shetland and in Sussex, and provided just enough pocket money to make this hobby possible. This is far from the only reason I'm grateful to them, but it's an important one.

Thank you to my editor, Simon Taylor, who showed enormous enthusiasm for this book from the moment it landed on his desk; to Chris Wormell, for his wonderful cover and chapter illustrations; and to the whole team at Transworld – especially Hayley Barnes, Marianne Issa El-Khoury, Oli Grant and Aoifé McColgan – who have made publication such an easy and enjoyable process. Thanks also to my agent, Jenny Brown, who could have tried to dissuade when I first mentioned wanting to write about angling, but who did exactly the opposite. Her support, as always, makes all the difference.

Thanks to the editors of *Fly Culture* and *Fallon's Angler*, who published earlier versions of 'The Back of Ronas Hill' and 'The Secret Loch' respectively.

Thanks to Sam Tongue, who provided useful feedback on a draft of the introduction; to Walter Wetherell, who offered encouragement at just the right moment; and to Tim James and Dr Andrew Herd, both of whom generously answered questions during the writing of this book.

Finally, thank you to Paddy, whoever he was. I will be forever grateful that he chose to take me and Rory fishing.

ABOUT THE AUTHOR

Malachy Tallack is the award-winning author of three books, most recently a novel, *The Valley at the Centre of the World* (2018). It was shortlisted for the Highland Book Prize and longlisted for the Royal Society of Literature Ondaatje Prize. His first book, *Sixty Degrees North* (2015), was a BBC Radio 4 Book of the Week, and his second, *The Un-Discovered Islands* (2016), was named Illustrated Book of the Year at the Edward Stanford Travel Writing Awards. As a singer-songwriter, he has released four albums and an EP, and performed across the UK. Malachy is from Shetland, and currently lives in Stirlingshire.

www.malachytallack.com
Twitter: @malachytallack